D0265001

ANCIENT SCOTLAND

ANCIENT SCOTLAND

NIGEL BLUNDELL

ACKNOWLEDGEMENTS

The publishers and the author would like to thank in particular three organisations whose assistance has made this book such a dramatic exposition of Scotland's glories, past and present. For research and for the generous use of photographs, we express our extreme gratitude to: Historic Scotland, the National Trust For Scotland, and the Scottish Tourist Board.

Photograph Page 1: *Dun Carloway broch, Isle of Lewis.*
Photograph Page 2: *Kilchurn Castle, Loch Awe.*

This edition first published in 1996 by the
Promotional Reprint Company Ltd,
Kiln House,
210 New Kings Road,
London SW6 4NZ.

ISBN 1 85648 371 1

Printed and bound in China

Contents

INTRODUCTION

The history of Scotland is much as its landscape . . . of peaks and troughs, of ruggedness and grandeur, of gentleness and calm splendour. Scotland is an incredible country. Its beauty is stunning. And the instant appeal of its countryside is matched by the warmth of its people.

But who are these people, the Scots? What makes them so different from their English neighbours just across a barely marked border? Why, around the world, do men and women cling to their Scottish ancestry in word, song and spirit? What strong cocktail created the nation of Scotland?

The very first inhabitants arrived when the ice retreated at the end of the last glaciation 9,000 years ago. It was a harsh terrain but they exploited the resources around them — gathering fruit, vegetables and shellfish, and fishing and hunting. We know they were here, these people of the Mesolithic Period, because they left behind the flint tools they used to hunt and to hew.

The first farmers arrived in the ensuing Neolithic Period. More than 5,000 years ago, before the Egyptians built their pyramids, these early immigrants were constructing houses, burial chambers and stone circles still standing today.

In the Bronze Age, from 2000 BC, a new, more sophisticated people arrived, using pots and beakers and ornamenting themselves. The landscapes that their agriculture created are still here — complete with plough marks and the remains of field boundaries — but buried beneath the present peat and topsoil.

In the Iron Age, from around 5000 BC, the tough subsistence lifestyle was matched by the savage nature of the peoples who fought for this land, and the relics that remain are of impregnable towers and fortified homes.

These people were all Scots — a name given to the country by one particularly influential tribe of invaders, the Celts of the western sea lanes. Their invasion was different in that it brought to Scotland the Gaelic language and the missionaries of Christianity.

Scotland has never been conquered — but has almost always been under siege. The invaders of the first millennium were the Romans, then the Vikings. In the second millennium they were the Normans and then, for bloody centuries, the English. And each invasive wave left its mark on the land, but more particularly on the people.

The other great influence on the Scottish people has been their environment: the terrain, its natural resources and the weather.

Scotland covers 7.2 million hectares (30,000 square miles), which is more than one-third of the total area of Great Britain. It lies between 55 and 60°N, with central Scotland on the same latitude as Moscow. Shetland, the most northerly group of islands, is closer to the Arctic Circle than to the south of England. Ireland is only about 20km (12 miles) away at its nearest point. Scotland's labyrinthine western seaboard is 416km (260 miles) long in a 'straight line', but over 3,200km (2,000 miles) along the indented coastline. And it has about 790 islands.

The seas on three sides of Scotland are comparatively warm, being part of the North Atlantic Drift which originates in the Gulf of Mexico. The seas are warmer than the land in winter, colder in summer. The result is a cool but equable climate, in spite of the northerly latitude. Yet only about a quarter of Scotland's countryside can be defined as 'improved' agricultural land. Much of the

rest, though poor for agricultural purposes, contributes to the country's famous scenic qualities.

So much for the bare statistics. The result, however, is a unique landscape, of which there are few so astonishingly beautiful, and few so rich in remains of the distant past.

The story of ancient Scotland which we tell in this book is one of a magical land and the various peoples to which it has played host — principally the Picts, the Scots, the Norsemen and the Britons. The sudden ascendancy of these four races, and their dramatically fluctuating fortunes and misfortunes, make a saga as astonishing as any in fiction.

Because the land has dictated the history of these peoples, so it is by the lie of the land that we must look at mankind's flimsy grip on a place that can be both harsh and inhospitable yet also lush and lovely. This book's journey through Scotland therefore takes place on two planes: time and space. So let's begin at the furthest point of the compass and at the most remote point in history. Let's begin by travelling far north to pick up Scotland's ancient story.

Above Left: *A reconstruction of an early farming settlement.*

Bottom Left: *Bronze Age man built many stone circles although their precise purpose is unknown — there are splendid examples at Brodgar and Stennes in Orkney and Callanish in Lewis.*

Above: *Night in a West Coast cave dwelling.*

Right: *Mesolithic hunting in South Edinburgh.*

TORRIDON

Torridon, in Ross & Cromarty, epitomises the grandeur and wildness of the Highlands. It includes some of Scotland's finest mountain scenery, including towering Liathach (1,053m/3,456ft) — the 'Grey One'. The spectacular 7km (4.5 miles) ridge of Liathach has two main peaks — Spidean a'Choire Leith (Peak of the Grey Corrie) and Mullaich an Rathain (Summit of the Row of Pinnacles)— and between them the narrow, exposed ridge of Am Fasarinen. The other two of the big three Torridonian mountains are Beinn Alligin (985m/3,230ft) and, on the north side of Loch Torridon, Beinn Eighe (1,010m/3,313ft). They are of red sandstone some 750 million years old; the tops are of white quartzite some 150 million years 'younger'.

There are 277 mountains in Scotland whose peaks rise above 3,000ft (compared, to only eight English). They were first catalogued by Sir Hugh Munro and 'bagging' them all has become a challenge to which many hillwalkers aspire.

Liathach's two peaks account for two of them: Beinn Eighe and Beinn Alligin two more. But these ancient, steep-sided hills can be tricky even for experienced climbers in winter when conditions can change rapidly as these pictures show.

Below: *In the middle of the year, glowering under a cloudy sky, Liathach has just a hint of snow at the peak.*

Right: *Liathach seen across Loch Clair on a clear winter's day perfect for walking. Beinn Eighe is to the right.*

Below right: *From the slopes of Beinn Eighe just in the snow, the scudding clouds hide most of Liathach as the weather starts to come in.*

ISLANDS AT THE END OF THE WORLD

The Shetland Islands are the most northerly point of Scotland. For thousands of years the Shetlands and their neighbours, the Orkney Islands, have been welcoming friendly visitors and, all too often, repelling the not so friendly. Some came by accident, others on planned expeditions — a mix of the wanderers, fishermen, traders, explorers, smugglers and invaders. All travellers.

In addition to the ships and the visitors who have stopped here to conquer, provision or languish, Shetland has provided a welcome landfall for many species of bird as they migrate between Africa and the Arctic Circle. The seashore, voes (small bays or creeks), moors and marshland have also served as a safe haven and animal habitat, the cliffs and rockscapes as footholds for wild plants and as breeding grounds for thousands of seabirds. They still do.

A full appreciation of the ancient history of the Shetland and Orkney Islands came only in the 19th century — and only then by the rude hand of nature . . .

During the 1890s violent storms broke into the low cliffs at Jarlshof, a small promontory near the southern tip of Shetland. The landowner, a Mr Bruce, dug into the sand and revealed a stunning maze of prehistoric structures.

The discovery at Jarlshof is a spectacular and enduring reminder of Shetland's heritage — and is regarded as one of the most fascinating and complex archaeological sites in all Britain. It was a settlement buried in time until the storm exposed the masonry of an entire village. Walls and hearths, wheel houses (circular homes) and Iron Age towers, all reflected the way of life of a long bygone age.

The first people to reach the Shetlands probably landed not far from Jarlshof some 5,000 to 6,000 years ago. The sea has risen since then, drowning and eroding the land, and the point where they beached their boats now lies probably a few metres below the sea and many metres offshore. Their arrival heralded the beginning of an intensive occupation of the site — from the earliest, primitive hunters to the more skilled agriculturalists, from the metal-working Beaker folk right up until the 17th century AD.

Jarlshof must have been a veritable crossroads of sea lanes. The Norwegian coast was only 48 hours away by sailing boat. From the hills around Jarlshof you can see Fair Isle, still one of the most isolated inhabited islands in Britain. (The intricate, colourfully patterned knitwear, which takes its name from the island, has today made Fair Isle famous worldwide.) And from Fair Isle can be seen the Orkney Islands, which lie between the Shetlands and Caithness, on the north coast of the Scottish mainland.

Jarlshof is an astonishing archaeological treasure chest and provides evidence of the scale of communal development of the ancient islanders, particularly during the comparatively 'recent' Iron Age. But what sort of domestic comforts did the very earliest inhabitants of this and other settlements enjoy?

Above: *The cliffs of the Orkneys are spectacular and none more so than those at Marwick Head which rise to a height of 300ft above the raging Atlantic waves.*

There are few clues to the lifestyles of the earliest islanders, except that we know the climate was kinder and the land therefore more arable in that period.

Before 4000 BC, people had begun to grow wheat and barley in Britain. Farmers had reached Shetland and Orkney before 3500 BC, and over the next thousand years built many tombs and settlements on the islands. They grew wheat and bere, an early form of barley still grown in Orkney today.

Their earliest dwellings were of wood. But when all the larger trees had been cut and used for construction, stone and turf became the standard building materials. In about 3500 BC the Neolithic farmers laid their dead in stone 'cists', one of which has been unearthed at Sumburgh, near Jarlshof. Although the dead were at first buried simply in stone-lined communal graves, soon the construction of more elaborate chambered tombs began. In Shetland these are comparatively small, with modest chambers which would have accommodated only a handful of burials. In Orkney, however, there are more substantial burial chambers.

These relics of the dead do not give many clues to the lifestyles of the living in this harsh, far-flung land. Here we are helped by an event which parallels the discovery at Jarlshof . . .

In the winter of 1850 a wild storm stripped the grass from the high dune known as Skara Brae, in the Bay of Skaill on mainland Orkney. An immense midden (or refuse heap) was uncovered. So too were the ruins of ancient dwellings. What came to light in that storm proved to be the best preserved prehistoric village in Northern Europe. And it remains so today.

Jarlshof sounds as if it gets its name from the Norse word Jarl, meaning earl. Certainly the Vikings lived there and they ruled the Northern Isles from the first Jarl of Orkney and Lord of Shetland, Sigurd Eysteinsson in the 10th century, through to the 15th century. But in reality the name is a modern invention attributed to Sir Walter Scott.

Before the Vikings came, Shetlands and Orkneys had thriving Bronze and Iron Age communities as can be seen from the two wonderfully preserved neolithic sites at Jarlshof (**Above Left**) *and Skara Brae* (**Above**).

The village of Skara Brae was inhabited before the Egyptian pyramids were built and flourished many centuries before construction began at Stonehenge. It is no less than 5000 years old.

But it is not its age alone that makes it so remarkable and so important. It is the degree to which it has been preserved. The structures of this semi-subterranean village survive in impressive condition. And so, amazingly, does the furniture in the village houses. Nowhere else in northern Europe are we able to see such rich evidence of how our remote ancestors actually lived.

They were careful planners and expert builders. The design of the village would have minimised heat loss, so that the houses could have been kept comfortably warm quite efficiently. A central hearth would have heated each house, as well as providing cooking facilities. The houses would have been very dark apart from the light radiating from the fire in the hearth. There are no surviving objects resembling lamps but it is quite likely that some form of lighting could have been employed by burning oil taken from marine mammals or sea birds. There would have been little ventilation, and the air inside the houses would have been very smoky. There would have been one benefit from this, however, in that food would have been smoked in the roof.

There was no knowledge of metal in the New Stone Age. People made their tools from stone — mainly from flint, although in Orkney and Shetland this was in short supply. So, while the tool kit of New Stone Age people elsewhere was largely made from stone, at Skara Brae it was from bone and wood. A great variety of tools not seen outside Orkney has been recovered from the site.

Gradually sand dunes formed around Skara Brae, separating the village from the sea — and eventually filling up and burying the buildings after they had been abandoned.

Another Orkney treasure is Maes Howe, built about 5,000 years ago. A large mound containing an entrance passage and burial chambers, it is the finest chambered tomb in north-west Europe. It is a remarkable mixture of simplicity and sophistication, its survival owed to the fine building stone used for it.

With the rings of standing stones at Brogar and Stenness, it is one of three great monuments at the heart of Orkney, where the power of a rich society was concentrated 5,000 years ago. Within a few miles of Maes Howe and the rings of standing stones were many other Neolithic and early Bronze Age structures, of which the chambered tombs at Knowe of Onstan or Unstan and at Wideford Hill and Cuween have survived to this day.

The Bronze Age (1800 to 600 BC) inhabitants of Orkney and Shetland experienced a steady worsening of climate which lost to arable farming the greater areas of the islands. Communal burials seemed to die out — perhaps the harsher living conditions did not allow enough time or surplus labour for the construction of elaborate cairns, and memorials seemed to take a simpler form.

Standing stones and stone circles are scattered through the northern and western islands of Scotland. Although they must have been associated with long-forgotten Bronze Age rituals, their precise purpose is unknown. There are splendid examples of these at Brodgar and Stennes, in Orkney, and at Callanish, in Lewis, in the

Western Isles. Further afield the most outstanding prehistoric monument in Scotland is probably the so-called Clava Cairns, five miles east of Inverness — circular burial chambers surrounded by standing stones and dating from before 2000 BC.

Eventually, the apparently peaceful lifestyle of the Bronze Age seems to have lapsed, and in the succeeding Iron Age (600 BC to AD 500) the islanders gathered themselves into more defensive communities. From about 500 BC the inhabitants of Shetland and Orkney began to build strong circular houses as the main dwellings of their farms. Gradually these became more sophisticated in design and formed the centres of small agricultural villages, frequently enclosed by outer defences in the form of ditches, banks or walls. There were also undefended settlements at this time, but these are less well studied. They are harder to locate than the massive structures known as brochs, for which the Northern Isles are famed.

Brochs are large stone-built towers. These imposing dry-stone structures, standing from 5m to 13m (16-42ft) high, were erected for defence by the Iron Age tribes of northern Britain. They are among the most ingenious and impressive military works of prehistoric man in western Europe and are unique to Scotland.

Until the 19th century, practically nothing was known about them. They were referred to as 'broughs' (defended places), 'Pict's castles' or 'Pict's hooses' by the local inhabitants and were so entered on the earliest Ordnance Survey maps until the end of the last century.

Essentially, a broch was a lofty, dry-stone tower, circular in plan with an immensely thick ring base enclosing a central courtyard. This was entered by a single passage originally provided with a wooden door halfway or so along its length.

From the central courtyard, openings gave access to chambers or 'cells' in or against the wall, and a doorway led to a stone staircase rising upwards within the wall thickness. This led upwards through a series of superimposed galleries, the ceiling of each forming the floor of the one above, emerging at the wall head, which commanded a view of the village, the outer defences and the countryside beyond.

Excavation evidence suggests that each broch may have had an inner structure of stone and wood. The surviving stone tower is to some extent merely a shell within which once sat the real dwelling place, possibly with one or more raised floors and covered by a thatched timber roof.

Because of collapse, the majority of the towers are reduced to mounds of grass-grown rubble covering the circular bases and wall stumps. The finest example of these unique structures is the Broch of Mousa in Shetland, which still survives to its original height of 13m (42m). At Mousa the visitor can see all the basic features which make up broch architecture. It stands on a natural rock bastion dramatically overlooking the sea. At nearby Clickhimin can be found the most extensively excavated example of brochs.

The nature of brochs was neatly summed up by the anonymous author of *Orkneyinga Saga*, written in the 12th or 13th century but telling tales of a far-distant past. Writing of the Broch of Mousa, which had been briefly reoccupied more than a thousand years after its construction, he wrote: 'It was an unhandy place to get at.'

When surrounded by outer ramparts and ditches, the brochs were manifestly unwelcoming to any predatory tribe. But impressive as they were, they were often merely the central points of more complex settlements. The broch was the residence of the principal

family of the community, and probably also served as a gathering place for communal activities ranging from meeting for war to entertainment on winter evenings. It also provided the last defensive resort of the community.

As brochs became widespread, they probably became indicators of the importance of the leading families of each community, so that no group was felt to be of significance in society unless it had a broch at the heart of its lands.

More than 500 broch sites are known or suspected. They are concentrated in Orkney, Shetland, the north mainland counties of Caithness and Sutherland, and in the Western Isles, with a few others in southwest and southeast Scotland. By around 100 BC there were more than 120 brochs on Orkney alone.

The people who built the brochs were farmers, successors to those who, many centuries before, had built the great chambered tombs of Orkney. Although they were in regular communication with other parts of Scotland, and perhaps ventured farther afield, there is no good evidence to suggest, as archaeologists once believed, that there was an invasion of 'broch builders' from outside the region.

The Iron Age farmers of Shetland, Orkney and the north Scottish coastline were, by the standards of northern Britain, prosperous and secure, with their mixed farming economy bolstered by the produce of the sea. They were probably well-connected, and trade or marriage would have brought fresh contacts, new ideas and innovative minds into the community. Orkney in the Iron Age was probably remarkably cosmopolitan.

Although considerable quantities of grain, mainly barley, were grown, farming was centred around the rearing of cattle, which provided meat, milk and leather. They may also have served as draught animals for ploughing. But more important, they represented wealth, and possession of cattle was probably the main index of social status, at least during the earlier Iron Age. There is some evidence that, as time went on, more 'modern' indicators of wealth also became current — like exotic jewellery.

Life would have been busy and work hard, but starvation can seldom have been a likely spectre for the Iron Age farmer. Long dark hours during the winter would have afforded time indoors to plan for the following season, weave and spin, tell tales and repair tools, fishing gear and boats. During the summer months much time was spent out of doors, with the late evenings perhaps enlivened by otter trappings along the shores or, for the more lawless spirits, forays to seek out and claim 'strayed' cattle.

So where did the broch builders, or rather their descendants, go? Probably not very far. The pattern seems to be one of slow drift away from the broch villages back to living in scattered farmsteads, once threat of attack was perceived to have disappeared. There is also evidence of a general reduction in population in the Shetland and Orkney Islands between the broch period and the arrival of Norse settlers around 800 AD.

Left and Below: *The Orkneys — no trees, just peat bogs, sea and a lot of wind. Indeed, you're never far from the sea or the wind in the Northern Isles: the highest gust of breeze ever in Britain was recorded in 1962 on the Shetland island of Unst — 177mph!*

The Ring of Brogar is one of the great monuments to the rich society which lived on the Orkneys 5,000 years ago.

Jarlshof — at the southernmost tip of the Shetlands' Mainland Island — is one of the most important archaeological sites in Britain, showing the development of civilisation from earliest times through to medieval days. It gives us an insight into how early settlements developed from the late Neolithic village through to the Bronze Age oval houses, Iron Age wheelhouse, Broch, Viking settlement and, finally, medieval farmhouse.

It must have been a hard life: while the Shetlands' average temperature rarely drops below 39°F, wind and proximity to the sea means that there haven't been trees on the islands for some time. Remains of tree stumps in the peat bogs show that once the climate was different but the weather has got colder and wetter and the winds have got stronger.

The pottery and metal artifacts were found during the extensive excavations.

Above Left: *An aerial view of Jarlshof showing its proximity to the sea and the extent of the excavations.*

Skara Brae

The wonderfully preserved Neolithic village of Skara Brae, on the west coast of Mainland Island, Orkneys, was excavated in 1928-30 by Australian archaeologist Vere Gordon Childe, professor successively at Edinburgh and London, then the expert on the Neolithic period and one of the leading archaeologists of the time. He found a complete stone-built settlement which, one theory suggests, was abandoned after a Pompeii style inundation — but for Vesuvius's volcanic ash and lava read the invasive fine sand that can be seen on the beach of the Bay of Skaill.

As on the Shetlands, proximity to the sea and substantial winds mean that the Orkneys have no wood for building or burning. The peat bogs solve the heating problems, but the lack of wood on the island meant that Skara Brae — like the comparable Neolithic site of Jarlshof on the Shetlands — was completely made of stone. The six or seven houses and a workshop hut were clustered together and linked by alleyways which would have been roofed over with stone

*The craftsmanship of the stonework shows the sophistication of the building techniques (***Far Left***) as do the interior furnishings and shelves (***Above*** and see photograph page 11).*

The main livelihood for the people of Skara Brae would have been the sea — their main source of food, although sheep and cattle were kept. That being said, there are distinctions apparently between Shetlanders and Orkadians: the former are fishermen with crofts and the latter crofters with boats

Brochs

While the usual theory of the purpose for the brochs is defensive — at a sign of danger the lookout on the top would sound the alarm and all the settlement's people and livestock would make for the security of the stone walls — there have been other theories. Many experts feel the size of the brochs precludes their use as a place of protection — they are just not big enough. One idea, proposed by the Orkneys' best-known writer, Eric Linklater, is that they were the structures upon which primitive catapults could have been placed to stop any invading foe before he reached the shores by sinking his boats.

*Whatever the real reason for the brochs, they are unique to Scotland and of the circa 500 brochs discovered so far, the best preserved are in the Northern Isles. Here (***Left, Below and Bottom***) Clickhimin Broch, Shetland, the best excavated of the brochs. The Broch of Mousa on Mousa Island to the east of Mainland is worth visiting too: its 40ft tower is almost intact.*

Right: *Gurness Broch. There are about 100 brochs in the Orkneys: they aren't as well preserved as those in the Shetlands except Midhowe and Gurness.*

THE WESTERN ISLES

The story of ancient Shetland and Orkney is paralleled by that of the Western Isles. This unique archipelago, otherwise known as the Outer Hebrides, is a beautiful, remote area — a chain of islands lying close to the northwest of Scotland, on the very edge of Europe and bordering the wide Atlantic Ocean. The combinations of land, sea and inland waters have produced landscapes of international importance.

The Western Isles stretch about 200km (130 miles) north-south from the Butt of Lewis to Barra Head, with the St Kilda group 22km (35 miles) to the west and lonely, uninhabitable Rockall a further 320km (200 miles) out into the North Atlantic.

The St Kilda archipelago is noteworthy in its own right. Remote and spectacular, it lies 176km (110 miles) from the Scottish mainland. A self-sufficient community lived there throughout ancient history. Fowling among the great colonies of sea birds (puffins for feathers and meat, young fulmars for oil and young gannets for meat) was the main employment, augmented by sheep herding, crofting and fishing. Its main island of Hirta maintained its population until 1930, when the islanders were evacuated at their own request.

By contrast, the islands of Lewis and Harris are combined like Siamese twins at the northern end of the Western Isles. They have been inhabited for more than 6,000 years but today only 30,000 people live on the 12 populated islands (Lewis and Harris, Bernera, Scalpay, Berneray, North Uist, Baleshare, Grimsay, Benbecula, South Uist, Eriskay, Barra and Vatersay). The people of the Western Isles are Gaels, bilingual Gaelic and English speakers.

The islands are formed from some of the oldest rocks in the British Isles. But despite this primeval ancestry, traces of the earliest inhabitants who set foot upon them are more elusive than in Shetland and Orkney. For much of the landscape of the Western Isles is relatively recent and is still changing.The reason is that the isles are generally low-lying and prone to blanketing by windblown sand. Remains of settlements from the Neolithic, Bronze and Iron Ages were generally sandwiched between sand dunes and the hinterland's more fertile uplands. Over the centuries, the drifting sands have alternately buried them and re-exposed them. For a brief while they may have stood crumbling by the shore — only to be finally swept away by the waves for ever.

These predations of the sea continue to the present day, with the comparatively recent settlement of Old Arnol, on Lewis, succumbing to the Atlantic breakers. While today only 12 islands support human habitation, yet the remains of post settlements, tombs and places of work and worship have been found on more than 50, many of them no more than dots on the map.

The principal monuments of the early Neolithic period, when farming first became established, are communal burial mounds, known as chambered cairns, and the great stone alignments and circles. Although excavations at the cairns of Uneval and Clettraval, on North Uist, have established that these great mounds of stone served as burial places, many questions remain. Were they repositories of the remains only of the tribal leaders? Since we know that the cairns were used over several centuries, how often were they cleared out and refurbished? And why are the cairns so concentrated in certain areas, particularly North Uist?

The Western Isles have standing stones aplenty: these two are on Arran in the Firth of Clyde. **Above** *Machrie Moor; there are Bronze Age burial chambers inside a stone circle on the moor.* **Right:** *Standing stone outside Brodick — the main village on the island where the ferry arrives.*

Then there are the standing stones and circles. Like the great chambered tombs, which generally predate them, they represent considerable feats of communal effort by a society where everyday life was a harsh battle with nature carried out around the humblest of stone homes of the most modest construction.

The group of about 20 intervisible standing stone sites around *Calanais* (in English Callanish), on the west coast of Lewis, represent the most varied collection in the whole of Britain — second only to Stonehenge in the United Kingdom for their grandeur.

The principal circle stands on a low ridge, visible for many miles. The plan is unique: a circle of 13 gneiss stones, up to 3.5m (11ft 6in) high, has a central stone 4.7m (15ft 5in) high. The circle is the terminus for a double row of stones leading north. Further single rows lead off the circle towards east, south and west. Apart from the circle and avenues of the main complex, the area boasts simple circles or near circles, arcs, alignments and single stones.

What was their significance? Although no one knows for cer-

tain, there is no doubt that some of the circles contain alignments with the heavenly bodies at specific times of the year. The rising and setting of the sun was obviously marked. And at Callanish the equinoxes and the winter and summer solstices seem to have been particularly significant events.

The Uists, Benbecula and Barra are rich with archaeological sites. North Uist contains some two-thirds of the chambered cairns found in the isles, with Barpa Langass, 8km (5 miles) from Lochmaddy, of particular importance. Settlement sites dating from the Neolithic and Bronze Ages have also been excavated at Northton on Harris, Loch Olabhat on North Uist, and Allt Chrisal on Barra. At these sites, small, oval, stone houses were surrounded by abundant broken pottery and midden material (domestic refuse that was allowed accumulate and rot before being spread on the fields). But apart from burial cairns and standing stones, very few sites or monuments dating before the Iron Age give us any insights into the domestic life of those who created them.

The social history of the Western Isles at the end of the Bronze Age and the beginning of the Iron Age (around 500 BC) is representative of the major changes wrought through the whole of Scotland. As we have seen in Shetland and Orkney, the new forms of settlement were designed for defence. Nowhere is this change more obvious than in the Western Isles where the archaeological record, almost empty for the Bronze Age, is represented in the Iron Age by more than a hundred fortified sites.

Clifftop promontories and islands in the middle of lochs were the natural choices. They would have been easy to fortify with a simple wall, and not too inconvenient for working the nearby fields or tending cattle. Perhaps these duns, as they are now called (from the Gaelic word for a fort), were temporary refuges. In time, however, they became permanent, with stouter walls and stone building. Access, originally by boat, was often provided by boulder causeways lying just below the surface and following a winding course to impede unwelcome visitors.

Eventually the fortifications were widened and heightened until they emerged as the classic Iron Age monument of the Scottish north and west: the broch. There is a theory that the brochs were designed by specialist builders who travelled around Scotland's Atlantic coast, contracting their skills to local communities. Just a few miles away from Callanish on Lewis stands one of these circular dry-stone fortified towers: the 2,000-year old Carloway Broch or Dun which is one of the best preserved examples of the few surviving brochs in the Western Isles.

By the time history came to be recorded, other structures appeared in the landscape: castles and religious buildings. Outstanding is Kisimul Castle on Barra, with its main tower dating from about 1120. Other castles, now ruined, include Borve in Benbecula and Ormacleit in South Uist. Teampull na Trionad (Trinity Temple), near Callanish in North Uist, dates back to the early 13th century, and the sites at Teampull Chalum Cille in Benbecula, and at Tobha Mor (Howmore), in South Uist, reflect these very early times. The chapels at Cille Barra are well preserved. But despite these later, perhaps more sophisticated structures, it remains a credit to those early dry-stone builders that the ancient duns and brochs of the Scottish northern coast and its islands continued to be occupied right up until the Middle Ages.

Above, Below and Right: *On the west coast of the Isle of Lewis, at Callanish at the head of East Loch Roag, stands the awesome collection of stone circles and avenues of standing stones called the 'Hebrides' Stonehenge'. Why early man spent so much of his time 4,000 years ago building these impressive monuments, no one knows for sure — although astronomical religious reasons seem the most likely. The more romantic legend says that the stones are actually giants whom St Kieran turned to stone for refusing to be baptised.*

STAFFA

The romantic and uninhabited island of Staffa lies seven miles west of Mull and six miles northeast of Iona. About half a mile long by a quarter of a mile wide, the 71-acre island is famous for its basaltic formations.

In fact Staffa was created at the same time and by the same volcanic activity as the Giant's Causeway on the north coast of Ireland. Celtic legend would have it that the causeway was built by the giant Fionn MacCaul who was known to the Scots as Fingal, and it is probable that the best known resultant feature of Staffa — Fingal's Cave — is named after him.

Immortalised by Mendelssohn in his celebrated Hebrides Overture, the cluster columns and seemingly man-made symmetry give the cave a cathedral-like majesty. Other famous visitors to the cave since its 'discovery' in 1772 by Sir Joseph Banks and a boat of scientists on their way to Iceland, have included Queen Victoria and Prince Albert, artist J.M.W. Turner, and poets and writers Keats, Wordsworth, Tennyson, Robert Louis Stevenson, Jules Verne and Sir Walter Scott.

Interestingly there is a town called Staffa on the shores of Lake Zurich. It was founded by one of Iona's monks who obviously had been struck by the sight of the island!

Below: *The structure of the closely packed hexagonal columns of basalt on Staffa is obvious in this photograph; they are formed by cooling within lava flows.*

ARRAN

During the Viking period, initiated in the area by a raid on Kintyre in AD 797, not only the Northern and Western Isles of Scotland but also the Isle of Man and much of Ireland came under Norse control. Arran, close to the shipping route between Norway and her subject kingdoms further south, and having in Lamlash Bay one of the best natural harbours in the west of Scotland, became an important base. For a time it formed part of the Norse kingdom of Man and Sudreyjar, the name 'Sudreyjar' denoting the whole of the Western Isles.

In 1156 Somerled, a chief of mixed Scottish and Norse descent, established a breakaway kingdom in the Isles, corresponding in area to the kingdom of Dalriada established by the Scots when they first came from Ireland. The 'kingdom' of the Isles was already being fragmented and absorbed into the neighbouring kingdom of Scotland when, in 1266, three years after the battle of Largs, Norway sold all the Western Isles to Scotland.

Right: *Glenashdale Falls plummet spectacularly 100ft down a lava sill.*

Below: *Standing stone on Arran's Machrie Moor.*

ST KILDA

Owned by the National Trust for Scotland, St Kilda, the most westerly of the main islands of the Outer Hebrides, lies 65km (41 miles) off North Uist open to the full force of the Atlantic. The pounding St Kilda has received from the oceanic breakers has led to substantial erosion and so the creation of stacks — and near vertical cliffs rising 1,000ft or more from the waves below. Inhabited until 1930, today there are only few people — the occasional (and strictly controlled) tourists or the soldiers at the early warning radar installation atop Mullach Môr (361m/1,184ft).

What St Kilda boasts is a half the British total of Puffins, possibly as many as 40 per cent of the world's gannets and sizeable colonies of Fulmars, Storm Petrels and Manx Shearwaters. Sheep left behind when the islanders departed have gone wild and survive in varying, seasonal quantities.

Above and Left: *Views of St Kilda village and walls.*

Right: *Stac Lee rises sheer from the Atlantic.*

Left: *The Isle of Lewis is the most populated of the Outer Hebrides and the largest, boasting the only Outer Hebridean town, Stornoway. On the west coast of Lewis is Arnol Black House Museum. With a thatched roof tied on with ropes, 6ft walls, no chimney and a central peat fire the Black House gives an excellent impression of life on the island in times gone by.*

Above: *Dun Carloway is on the west coast of the Isle of Lewis overlooking East Loch Roag. It is a substantial and well preserved broch with nearly 22ft of walls in places and a substantial diameter of 47ft.*

Right: *Inscriptions or ornamentation from Carn Ban, a 100ft long chambered cairn dating from the neolithic period.*

OUTPOST OF THE EMPIRE

The Iron Age in Scotland lasted until relatively recent times; it is generally regarded as stretching from 500 BC to AD 560. It is a period that saw the incursion of the Roman Empire through mainland Britain and, of course, the advent of Christianity. Yet in material terms, the northern and western islands have little to show for these global changes. Forts, duns, brochs and wheel houses continued to be adapted and occupied. Archaeologists have discerned only minor changes in the pottery of the northern inhabitants of Scotland — and the few exotic items that might have assisted them in dating sites have been imported from other regions.

The influence of the Roman Empire fell far short of these northern realms, although legend has it that they explored the seas as far as the Shetland Islands. They certainly knew of a cluster of 100 islands at the confluence of the North Sea and the North Atlantic. They called them 'Ultima Thule'.

But to see the effect of this new civilisation transplanted from the Mediterranean to the chill climes of Scotland, we must move south from the mysterious Celtic seascapes of the broch builders to the Lowland moors and plains. For its was here in the 1st century AD that the Roman legions — which had landed in southeast Britain, conquered and subdued the whole of England — marched into Scotland. Incidentally, it is only from this period that we come across the first written records of Scottish history.

In AD 81 Gnaeus Julius Agricola, governor of the Roman province of Britain, invaded southern Scotland with Legio IX Hispana and advanced to a front-line position betwixt the estuaries of the Rivers Clyde and Forth — a line that today would link the cities of Edinburgh and Glasgow. In Lothian stands a 2.7m (9ft) tall sandstone monolith, known variously as the Caiy Stone, Kel Stone and General Kay's Monument, which traditionally marks the site of a battle between the Picts and the Romans.

Agricola built a chain of forts across the land and threw forward one major bastion at Stirling, which he made his headquarters. Sustained by the Roman fleet, which matched his progress along the sinuous eastern coastline, in AD 83 Agricola vanquished the local Caledonians in the battle of Mons Graupius, believed to be the Hill of Moncrieffe.

We know of these events from the writings of the Roman historian Tacitus, who happened to be Agricola's son-in-law. Tacitus wrote proudly of his relation's victories, principally against the Caledonian chieftain Calgacus, but criticised subsequent Roman strategy. For in AD 84, only months after Agricola had subdued the Lowland tribes, the general received sudden orders from Rome to withdraw. As Tacitus wrote: '*Perdomita Britannia et statim omissa*' (Britain is conquered then is at once thrown away).

Imperial strategy became defensive rather than offensive. The Emperor Hadrian himself visited Britain in AD 121 and ordered the building of the famous Hadrian's Wall as a deterrent to the raiding parties of the factionalised northern tribes. Bits of it still stand today between the estuaries of the Solway and the Tyne — a line back into England and far south of Agricola's earlier frontier.

Above: *Rough Castle is one of 13 forts built by the Romans and so far found along the Antonine Wall. At less than an acre in size, it would not have housed a major unit.*

Right: *The Caiy Stone in Lothian traditionally marks the site of a battle between the Roman legions and the Picts.*

Less than 20 years later, however, new Emperor Antoninus Pius ordered the restoration of Roman rule over the defiant northerners. Within months of succeeding Hadrian in AD 138, the tough new emperor decided to abandon Hadrian's Wall, which was still being modified, and move the frontier north some 160km (100 miles) and to reoccupy Lowland Scotland. The then governor of Britain, Lollius Urbicus, was given the task of pushing the frontier of Rome back to Agricola's advanced positions.

The Antonine Wall was constructed during the years following AD 142. The new wall was built across the narrow waist of Scotland formed by the Rivers Forth and Clyde and their tributaries the Carron and the Kelvin. It ran for exactly 40 old Roman miles (about 37 modern miles or 60km) from present Bowness on the

Forth to Old Kilpatrick on the Clyde, following for most of its length the southern slopes of the central valley of Scotland.

The Antonine Wall was a less permanent structure than Hadrian's earlier wall, perhaps reflecting the Roman Imperial Army's manpower shortages. It had a stone and turf rampart base 4.3m (14ft) wide and almost as high, topped by timber. In front of the rampart was a deep ditch, the earth from which was tipped onto the north side to form a further mound. At intervals of about 3.5km (2 miles) along the wall were forts, some housing small detachments but others designed for major forces, linked by a military road and beacon-platforms. And between the forts (Rough Castle, some 5km (3 miles) west of Falkirk, is a well-preserved example) lay still more outposts, each garrisoned by up to 30 men.

These soldiers, all highly trained, were charged with the task of defending the province of Britain. Most of the summer they would have spent north of the wall patrolling the central Lowlands, chasing off raiders and supervising the local tribes. Recruits for the maintenance of the Antonine Wall would have been mainly local in origin. For like the Britons in the south, the Pictish-Scottish inhabitants of the agricultural Lowlands were now beginning to learn the long, slow lesson of living as neighbours with the Romans. The best preserved remains of a Roman fort, at Bearsden, reveal the domestic, as well as military, lifestyle of an army whose area of operations extended from the Clyde to the Euphrates.

It was under the Emperor Severus and his son Caracalla that the Roman Empire arranged a peace on its northernmost boundary which would last in the main for 200 years. During the war Severus had fought to win the his position, the Roman armies had been pulled away from frontier duties in Britain and the northern tribes

had overrun the weakened defences. Severus had to conduct the campaigns of reconquest himself, invading Scotland in AD 208. He died at his headquarters in Eboracum (York) and was succeeded by Caracalla who brought the war to a conclusion. The peace centred on the Wall of Hadrian with strong outposts as far north as Carpow on the Tay from which a large garrison of Legio VI and II Augusta patrolled the area.

As the history of the Roman Empire became one of civil war and wars of succession, the British legions played their part, leaving the province to fight on the Continent but each time they returned to reconquer lands taken in their absence by the Pictish tribes. By the end of the 4th century, Hadrian's Wall had become the frontier again and the farther outposts in Scotland abandoned. As troubles closer to home caused the empire to contract, one by one the legions were recalled from Britain to defend Italy and Rome herself from the Goths. By AD 430 not only Scotland but the whole of Britain had been abandoned for the final time.

The departure of the Roman legions did not bring peace to Scotland. The reverse occurred. At first the Caledonian tribes, growing ever bolder, pushed further and further south — but they soon encountered a mass movement of humanity that was exploding upon the British Isles in the vacuum left by the retreating Romans. Teutonic invaders, the Angles and the Saxons, held back for so long by the Roman east coast forts, swarmed across the North Sea and drove the native Britons westwards and northwards into southern Scotland. The native Scots also had to watch their back, because Saxon raiders were establishing a hold on the east coast.

The history of Scotland was about to take yet another, dramatic turn.

Above Left: *Aerial view of Rough Castle.*

Below Left: *A depression in the ground, a piece of wall, a section of ditch: not much remains of the northern boundary of the Roman Empire.*

Below: *Defensive positions around Roman encampments used what were called 'lilies' — pits dug to a depth of about three feet with sides which tapered slightly towards the bottom where fire-hardened, sharpened stakes were projecting from the bottom. The pits were then covered with brushwood to hide the trap.*

Left: *Croy Hill Fort is to the west of Rough Castle separated along the Antonine Wall by forts at Westerwood and Seabegs. The ditch in front of the wall was about 12m (40ft) wide and 3.75m (12ft) deep although at Croy Hill there is a patch of rock which defeated even the patient professionalism of the legions.*

Right and Below: *The wall started at Old Kilpatrick on the Clyde and there was a fort — Duntocher — between the start and Bearsden. These two photographs show the Bearsden bath house — always an important part of any Roman establishment. Every permanent fort had its bath house which consisted of a series of rooms of varying temperatures and humidity.*

INVASION OF THE NORSEMEN

It is worth here pausing to re-examine the racial mix that was Scotland in the first half of the first millennium.The ancient inhabitants of Scotland were Celts, who had sailed across the seas and settled in these northern lands in a series of minor migrations stretching back to 1000 BC and beyond. By Roman times, Scotland was divided between four main races — the Picts, Britons, Teutonic Anglo-Saxons and the Scots.

The most powerful of these were the Picts who reigned supreme from Caithness in the north to the Forth in the south. Of Celtic stock, some historians say they originally arrived from the continent of Europe as part of the Celtic migration to the British Isles during the first millennium before Christ. Others say they were of Scythian origin.

The neighbouring Britons of the Strathclyde region were another Celtic race, speaking a kindred tongue and controlling the area stretching from the Clyde to the Solway and beyond into Cumbria. The Teutonic Anglo-Saxons, who hailed from lands lying between the mouth of the Rhine and the Baltic, occupied the country south of the Forth and controlled an area stretching southwards into Northumbria.

Finally, to the west, embracing what is now Argyll, Kintyre and the neighbouring islands, lay the Scots. This warlike Celtic race from Dalriada in northern Ireland had arrived in force in the 3rd century AD and began colonising a sister kingdom of Dalriada in an area roughly coincident with the old counties of Argyll and Bute.

The Scots found themselves at first overshadowed by the Picts. But as Roman influence waned in the north of Britain — at this time known as Alba or Alban — the Celtic newcomers pressed their advantage and filled the vacuum. Although Picts and Scots occasionally joined forces to harass the Romans, the Scots' first loyalties were to their fellow men across the sea in Irish Dalriada. Their conflict with the Picts was to take several hundreds years and the spilling of much blood before it was resolved.

When they sailed across the sea from Ireland, they brought their culture to lands less remote than those we have so far visited — to the hospitable peninsulas and shore hugging isles of the central west coast, like Arran and Iona. They first brought with them the Gaelic language and in due course gave Scotland its present name. They also heralded an extraordinary new cultural 'invasion' — Christianity.

Of its effects on Scotland, and the gloriously rich architectural heritage it has left, we shall learn in a later chapter. Meanwhile, however, we must examine an invasion that was less welcome, less gentle — but which eventually embraced Christianity and helped spread it not only around Scotland but the known world.

In the 9th century AD, the whole western world was rocked by the movement of Norsemen away from their own countries, their longships leaving the fjords for new lands across the sea. Their adventuring and colonisation in time took them south to the Holy Land and west to Greenland and almost certainly North America. The Scandinavians arrived in Britain in force shortly before AD 800. Not only the Northern and Western Isles and Caithness, but also the Isle of Man and much of Ireland and eventually England, succumbed to these forays, and the predominantly Pictish inhabitants were forced to give way to this powerful force. To pick up the earliest threads of the story of the feared and fearless men from Scandinavia, we must return to the far north of Scotland. Back to now-familiar Jarlshof, in Shetland, that extraordinary time capsule which, as we have learned, is a mere two days' sail by Viking longboat from the coast of Norway.

In the 9th century the Shetlands became an important link in the raiding and migration routes 'west over sea' to Britain, Ireland, Iceland and Greenland. Between AD 830 and 860 Kenneth MacAlpin united the Picts and Scots and it was probably after Pictland became Scotland that the Norsemen first settled at Jarlshof. The earliest known Scandinavian burials in the Scottish islands date to the latter half of the 9th century.

It has been suggested that the first Norse settlers in Scotland came from the More-Trondelag district of Norway, and that later settlers came from the districts of East and West Agder. It does appear that the people who came to Shetland and Orkney hailed from at least some part of southern Norway.

From 872 AD, a Viking earldom was established in Orkney. Not only warriors but farmers and their families came and stayed, bringing with them a new and enduring culture. Wherever the Vikings went, they took their law and their language. In the Western Islands of the Outer Hebrides, the place names are almost all of Norse origin. The Vikings invaded and settled the islands from the 9th century onwards and it was not until 1280 that Norway handed the Western Isles over to the kingdom of Scotland under the Treaty of Perth.

Equally, of Shetland's 50,000 place names, the vast majority are 'Norn'. The local parliament was held at Lawting Holm, an islet in Tingwall Loch. Enduring folklore and sagas are associated with many other legendary sites, such as the Broch of Mousa, the Loch of Girlsta, Haroldswick on Unst, the 'Bears Bait' on Fetlar, and the beach at Gulberwick. The latter is the site of the wrecking of two longships of Norse ruler Earl Rognvald Kali as they were on their way to the Crusades in the 12th century.

For it is a myth that the Norsemen were Vikings intent on only 'rape and pillage'. The Christian ethos was strong in the islands. The *Orkneyinga Saga* tells us that Earl Rognvald Kali gathered crusaders together in Orkney in 1150. After wintering on the islands — not without squabbles over money and love affairs — they sailed for Jerusalem. While the earl was away rivals struggled for mastery over the islands. One of the claimants, Harold Maddadarson, son of the Earl of Atholl, tried a surprise attack on Orkney. On 6 January 1153 he landed at Stromness and marched eastward; caught by a storm he and his men took shelter for three days in Maes Howe. Two of his men went mad there. But they were not the only Vikings to enter the tomb. The proof is in the runes Earl Rognvald's men and women carved when they returned from the crusade later in 1153.

The 'City and Royal Burgh of Kirkwall', capital and administrative centre of the Orkney Islands, is one of the best preserved examples of an ancient Norse settlement, being mentioned in the *Orkneyinga Saga*. Founded around 1035 by Earl Rognvald Brusson, Kirkwall's name comes from the old Norse 'Kirkjuvagr' meaning 'church-bay'. This is a reference to a church much older than the present cathedral that dominates the town.

St Magnus's Cathedral was founded in 1137 by Earl Rognvald

Far Left: *Viking graffiti from Maes Howe. It's evident from what's written on the walls of the tomb that Vikings ransacked it: 'Haakon alone bore the treasure out of this tomb', says one. 'Thorny was bedded. Helgi says so', says another. It seems that the urge to deface is not confined to modern aerosol wielding youth!*

Above Left: *Illustrations from Jarlshof on stone and slate of Viking longboats. It may seem hard to believe that Norsemen went to the Holy Land on crusade but they actually went even farther than that. The Varangian Guard of the tsars of Kievan Russia were Vikings who probably reached Kiev via the Black Sea.*

Above: *Inside the chambered cairn of Maes Howe on Orkney.*

Below: *Steatite (soapstone) lamp from Jarlshof.*

Kolson to the memory of his uncle, St Magnus. Built of local red and yellow sandstone more than 850 years ago, it was at the time one of Europe's great architectural achievements. Today, weathered but untouched by pollution, it is still bright and clean.

Viewed today, Kirkwall's main street is little changed in centuries: a narrow, winding thoroughfare that echoes the shape of the shoreline. And Viking influence is still remarkably prevalent in the northern islands. Even though Orkney was sold to Scotland in 1468, there are still lingering loyalties — as Kirkwall's stone houses annually echo to such celebrations as Norwegian Constitution Day!

Equally, Scandinavian rule in Shetland was to last for more than 600 years until the mid-15th century, when the islands were finally given as a dowry to Scotland. As a reminder of this heritage, the Shetland capital of Lerwick annually holds a midwinter festival known as 'Up Helly Aa'. This spectacular celebration features a procession of 1,000 torch-carrying revellers, a squad of Vikings in horned helmets and full regalia, and a longship dragged through the streets of Lerwick before its ceremonial burning.

Above and Top Right: *Jarlshof, showing the size of the site and the remarkable state of preservation of the buildings.*

Right and Far Right: *The Brough of Birsay is a small island off the northwest of Mainland Island, in the Orkneys. From it, Norse jarls ran an empire which — at its peak under Earl Thorfinn the Mighty in c1100 — controlled the Northern Isles, the Western Isles, a large part of northern Scotland and much of Ireland. On the Brough remains can be seen of a palace, cathedral, houses (as illustrated* **Far Right***) and other things like this cross-inscribed grave slab (***Right***). Thorfinn's grandson, Magnus Erlendsson, was canonised following miracles at the site of his murder and his body, with an axe wound in the skull, has rested ever since in St Magnus Cathedral in Kirkwall, which was founded in his memory.*

Above and Right: *The Broch of Mousa is the best preserved of all the brochs and shows to great effect how imposing and substantial these buildings were. It is on a small island to the east of Sandwick on the southern peninsula of Mainland in the Shetlands. The aerial view shows clearly the double skin which allows for rooms and an inner courtyard. As a defensive establishment the broch would certainly have been difficult to penetrate and Mousa is mentioned in Norse sagas as being strong enough to withstand Viking raids. Mousa Broch is still 12m (40ft) tall and before gunpowder it would certainly have been a difficult nut to crack.*

Left: *Pottery from Jarlshof. The Norse occupation of Jarlshof saw major building work. At first a 21m (70ft) rectangular stone farmhouse was erected and later extended; a long house was added subsequently as was a third farmhouse.*

LANGUAGE

In 10th century Scotland, the principal language was Gaelic. In the last thousand years, its use has contracted first becoming the language of the Highlands, then in recent times losing even more ground to English as the Highlands emptied of its native population.

Today Gaelic has its stronghold in the Western Isles, where it remains a vigorous force in written and spoken prose and poetry. However, it is in place names all over Scotland that it will be most apparent to the visitor — each craggy outcrop or lowering loch has its usually descriptive Gaelic name.

Gaelic	English
aber, abhair	river mouth or confluence
achadh	field
ard, aird	high point
allt	burn, river
ban	white
beag	small
bealach	pass
bodach	old man
buachaille	shepherd
buidhe	yellow
cam	bend, bay
caol, caolas	strait (cf kyle)
chailleach	old woman
coille	wood
coire	cauldron, or corrie
dearg	red
dubh	black
drochaid	bridge
drum, druim	ridge
garbh	rough
gobhar	goats
gorm	blue
kin, ken (ceann)	head
liath	grey
lomond	beacon
meall	round hill
mor	big
ros, ross	promontory or moorland
stob	top, peak
tigh	house
uig	bay
uisage	water

Scotland's other language is Scots, a form of 'English' which has grown from a Northumbrian dialect of Anglo-Saxon. Scots has absorbed French, Germanic and Norse influences and was the standard speech of court until James VI of Scotland inherited the English crown in 1603 and moved to England.

From then on, it also lost ground — never, for example, gaining a standard mode of spelling. This process was accelerated by the King James Bible being printed in English but not Scots. Finally with the Union of Parliaments in 1707, English became the official language of administration.

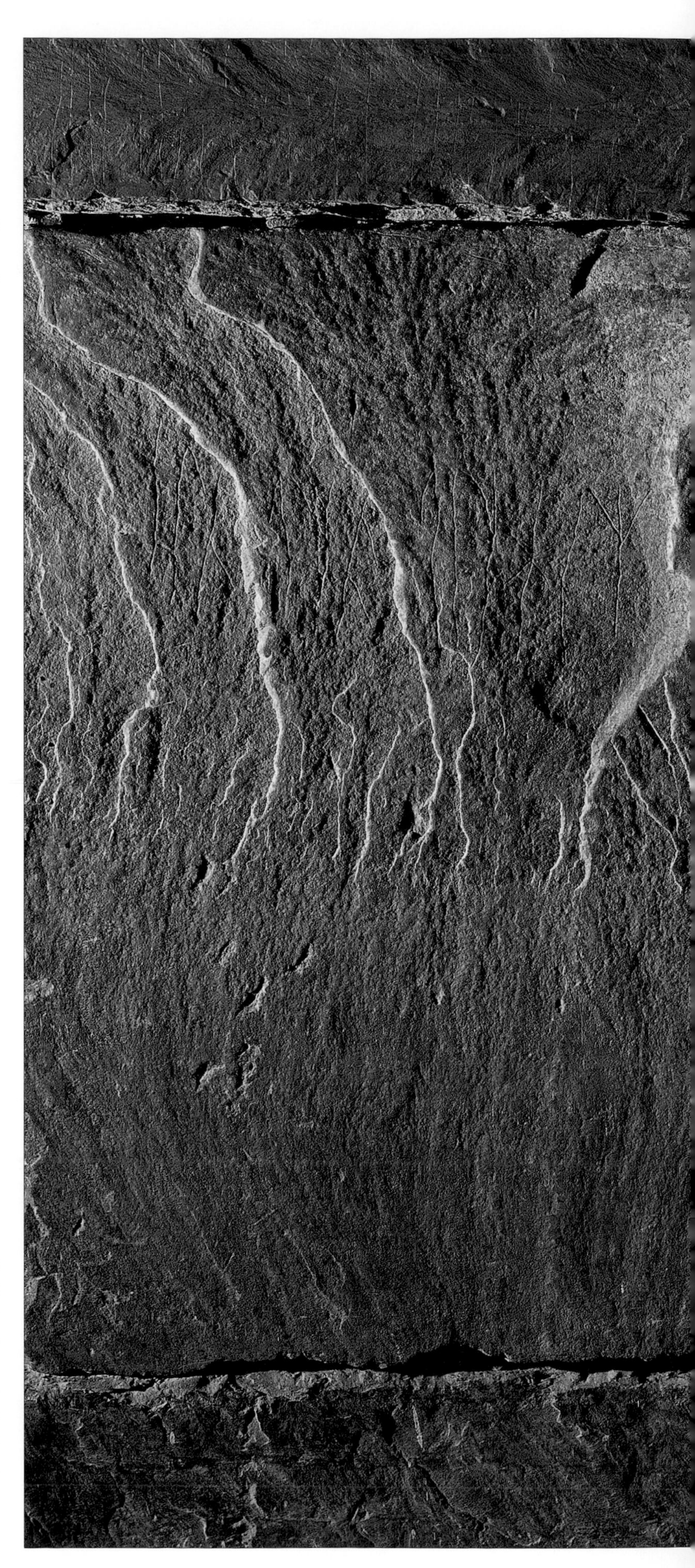

Right: *Viking writing — runes on the wall at Maes Howe.*

THE NORMAN CONQUEST

Much had occurred in England in the early days of the second millennium. In 1066 King Harold resoundingly crushed a renewed Viking offensive in north-eastern England, then marched his exhausted troops south to the Sussex coast where yet another invasion force was challenging his supremacy. The resultant Battle of Hastings — between King Harold's Anglo-Saxons and the northern French invaders of King William of Normandy — was the single most important turning point in the 'recent' history of the British Isles. For when, after a closely fought conflict, Harold was carried dead from the field of battle, the spoils of war fell to a French-speaking hierarchy who changed the old British lifestyle, language and culture for ever.

A chain of vast fortifications was thrown up across the land to maintain the Norman overlords' stranglehold on the recalcitrant islanders. It took many decades before the Normans could finally claim to have subdued their newly conquered lands.

When the Normans ventured to the north of the British Isles, they found a people who were, for the first time in its history, coming together almost as one nation. It was under the rule of Duncan, King of Strathclyde (1034-40), that we can first speak of the kingdom of Scotland. Indeed, it had virtually the same borders as it does today. Duncan was killed by Macbeth, who successfully ruled Scotland for 17 prosperous years, to be succeeded in 1057 by one of Scotland's most significant early monarchs, Malcolm III.

There was some uneasy unity when Malcolm took the throne. Most commonly known as Canmore, a Gaelic name literally translated as 'big-head', Malcolm married Margaret of the royal house of Wessex, giving him some interest in the English throne. But when William the Conqueror finally invaded Scotland in 1071, he forced Malcolm to pay homage to him at Abernethy. In the intervals between the fighting, amicable relations were maintained between England and Scotland, for Malcolm remained a popular figure at the English court. But his death in 1093, while raiding Alnwick, in Northumberland, plummeted Scotland into 30 years of turmoil, ruled over by a succession of weak, insecure kings.

The first of these was Malcolm's 60-year old brother Donald Ban. Donald clashed with William Rufus, the new king on the English throne, who made several attempts to usurp him. Donald's half-brother Edgar became king in 1097, followed by his brother Alexander in 1107. Alexander married King Henry I's daughter and his sister Maud became the wife of the king himself. Ties with England grew closer and the Norman influence even greater.

When Alexander died in 1124, he was succeeded by his brother David, the ninth son of Malcolm and already the ruler of most of southern Scotland. He was to reign for 30 years. Like his brothers, David had been brought up in England where he had had a Norman education and made many Norman friends. In addition to being King of Scotland, he was also Prince of Cumbria. Further, by his marriage to a rich Norman heiress, he held the title Earl of Northampton and Huntington. Because of this he was one of the most powerful barons in England as well as being the English king's brother-in-law. He was also to prove one of the most innovative of Scotland's early kings.

On returning to Scotland, David began distributing large estates amongst his Anglo-Norman friends and associates who then became landowners on both sides of the border. At the same time, David introduced something akin to a feudal system of ownership to the Lowlands of Scotland. In the Highlands, however, the king's ideals counted for little while the Northern and Western Islands and some coastal regions gave a loose allegiance to Norway.

David did his best to establish a national system of justice and administration with a specially selected governing body to advise him. He appointed sheriffs to administer justice. He also encouraged trade with foreign countries and established two royal mints and a standard system of weights and measures. David granted the status of burgh to a number of towns, together with a freedom from tolls and the right to hold markets and fairs. He was a devout man and established more parishes, built more churches and endowed monasteries. He died in 1153, ending a rule which had brought with it dramatic change.

The focus of this short narrative of Scotland's ancient history now turns to its central heartlands — to Stirling, the 'crossroads' of the nation. Set at the highest navigable point of the Forth, and on the line of the main pass through the northern hills, Stirling guarded both the principal north-south and east-west routes across Scotland. The coincidence of strategic significance and a naturally strong site meant that the great rock upon which old Stirling stands was a prehistoric fortress and the likely site of the city of Iudeu, which figures in accounts of British kings in the 7th century.

However, Stirling Castle does not begin to appear in recorded history until the early 12th century, by which time it is already a residence of Malcolm's Canmore dynasty. Alexander I had founded a chapel here, and probably died within the walls of the castle in 1124. The castle next comes on record exactly 50 years later, when it was handed over to Henry II of England, along with five other castles, to pay for Scottish King William the Lion's release after his capture at the battle of Alnwick. Scottish control of Stirling was regained in 1189, and 25 years later King William died within it.

In all this time, we have no idea of Stirling Castle's physical appearance, although most of the buildings would have been of

Right: *Old Scone Palace was the spot to which Kenneth MacAlpin is said to have brought the Stone of Destiny. Generations of Scottish monarchs were crowned on it until it was taken to London by Edward I: it has resided in the coronation chair at Westminster since although recently it has been mooted that the stone will be returned North of the border. Scone Palace today is a castellated mansion enlarged in 1802-13 around 16th century and earlier buildings. It is the home of the Earls of Mansfield whose family has owned the property since it was given to Sir David Murray by James VI after 1600.*

timber. The castle probably began to assume more permanent masonry from the late 13th century — something the turmoil of the succeeding century was to obliterate.

Edward I of England was the scourge of the Scots. Nicknamed 'Longshanks', he had long coveted the Scottish kingdom. As one of the most important castles in the kingdom, Stirling naturally played a major part in the Scottish struggle for independence of English overlordship. In 1291 Edward I took custody of all Scottish royal castles while he adjudicated on who was the rightful king of Scotland, and the castle's history over the next 50 years is mainly that of a struggle for its occupation by the forces fighting on behalf of the rival claimants. During the course of this struggle, Stirling was the scene of several of the finest triumphs of the Scottish patriots — although the benefits derived from these triumphs were short-lived.

In 1297 an army led by that great Scottish hero William Wallace overthrew the English in a famous victory at Stirling Bridge, and thus secured the castle for a time. Wallace was forced to defend his victor's crown the following year at Falkirk, and this time Edward I wrought his revenge. The English and Welsh archers shot down the Scottish foot and so enabled a charge by Edward's heavy cavalry to prove decisive.

By 1304 Stirling was the only castle left to the patriots. In that year Edward I instigated a successful siege, using fire-throwing equipment and a siege machine known ominously as the 'War Wolf'. The castle was again in English hands. The country seemed to lie at his mercy. And when the Scots' champion Wallace was captured and put to death at the king's orders in London in 1305, hope ran out and final surrender seemed inevitable.

Scotland was occupied from end to end and a foreign garrison lay in every town from Annan to Dingwall. Yet some did not despair and, in 1306, Robert the Bruce was crowned King of Scots at Scone, with a mission to recover his kingdom and regain freedom for his subjects. For the victories won by the first Edward were not followed up by his son. In the years which followed the tide slowly turned, almost imperceptibly at first and then with gathering impetus, to the chagrin of Longshanks's successor, Edward II. One by one the towns and fortresses were retaken until by the spring of 1314, of only three castles which were still in English hands, Stirling remained the most important.

In that year, Stirling Castle was under siege by a Scottish force commanded by King Robert's brother, Sir Edward Bruce. Extraordinarily, under the laws of chivalry of the day, an agreement had been made between Edward Bruce and the English governor of Stirling castle, Sir Philip Moubray, whereby it was to be surrendered if not relieved before Midsummer Day (24 June 1314).

Edward II of England, realising the blow that failure would mean to his prestige, determined to relieve the castle in time. In doing so, he believed that he could draw the main Scots army out to oppose him, rather than allow them to conduct the campaign by their previous, highly successful guerrilla tactics. With one mighty stroke, Edward felt that he could recover all the ground lost since his father's death. Robert the Bruce was made aware of the English king's intentions by March 1314 — and determined to accept the challenge.

Above: *William Wallace's statue at the entrance to Edinburgh Castle.*

Left: *Strategically placed on the main communication and trade route south, Stirling Castle was the most important piece of real estate in Scotland in medieval times. It had to withstand sieges by both Scots and English as it changed hands in the 13th and 14th centuries. In more peaceful times the castle changed from fortress to royal residence and from the late 15th, through the 16th centuries it was used heavily by the Stuart kings. Illustrated is the Renaissance south façade of King James V's Palace which can be seen behind the crenellated curtain-wall built by James IV, his father. The end result of these building works was an important early classical exterior outside and sophisticated royal apartments inside.*

Right: *The Wallace Monument — the arousal of interest in Wallace caused by the film* Braveheart *is not the first time he has been hero-worshipped from beyond the grave. The Victorians went to town over this romantic hero and the epitome of this can be seen in this 67m (220ft) stone structure perched atop a rocky outcrop near Stirling. It was completed in 1870.*

ONE PEOPLE, ONE NATION

The dramatic set-piece battle which followed was probably the greatest which ever took place on Scottish soil. It is known to all Scots as the Battle of Bannockburn and to the English of earlier days as the Battle of the Pools, or sometimes as the battle near the Bannock Burn, near Stirling. In Gaelic the battle is known as *Blar Allt a Bhain-chnuic* or 'the Battle at the Burn of Bannock'. By this clash of armies, Scotland was to win its independence from England — at least temporarily — on 23 and 24 June 1314.

Edward had already sent out summonses to the English counties, to Wales and Ireland, for levies and he ordered the army to concentrate at Wark on the Tweed, near Berwick, by 10 June. The army, led by Edward himself, consisted of 2,000 heavy cavalry, and upwards of 17,000 archers and foot.

The cavalry was furnished by the nobles, knights, squires and landowners, all with their own paid men-at-arms. The horsemen wore chain-mail and armour, bore a 3.6m (12ft) lance and had a mace or battleaxe as a close combat weapon. The horses, some with light armour, were gorgeously equipped with flowing blankets, known as 'trappers', their function being to trap or entangle swords and spear thrusts. Edward was relying for victory on the charge of this mass of heavy cavalry which was accustomed to strike terror into the hearts of any but the most highly trained and disciplined body of foot.

The archers carried a long bow, a quiver with 24 arrows and in addition they had a short sword or dagger as a personal weapon. The foot soldiers were spearmen, each carrying a 3.6m (12ft) spear, a shield and a sword or dagger.

By contrast, Robert the Bruce is believed to have had only about 5,500 trained men to meet the English army of nearly 20,000. The Scottish soldier bore a 3.6m (12ft) spear, a sword, axe or dirk as a personal weapon, and carried a targe or shield. Bruce's few archers provided a longbow and 24 arrows. His horsemen were organised into a small body of some 500 light cavalry, under Sir Robert Keith.

As a kind of reserve, a goodly number of the 'small folk', often erroneously called gillies or even camp followers. These 'small folk' were minor tenant farmers, townspeople, labourers and craftsmen who had joined to strike their blow for Scotland , but whom Bruce wisely kept out of his divisions because of their lack of equipment, training and discipline. They were even expected to supply their own arms. Despite this, the numbers of these 'small folk' gradually increased to some 2,000 as small parties of clansmen joined from remote areas.

The fact that nobles, knights, landowners and tenant farmers fought together, with their men on foot, made for a high standard of leadership, cohesion, training and discipline. In the English army, by contrast, most of the natural leaders were serving together in the cavalry and the infantry felt the loss.

On 23 June, Bruce, unarmoured, and mounted on a sturdy

Above: *Could there be anything more fearsome than a charge of heavily armoured knights? At Bannockburn the charge was halted and the Bruce won the day.*

Right: *King Robert I and his second wife. His daughter Marjory married Walter Steward of Scotland and their son became Robert II, the first Stuart king.*

Scottish pony, was riding round his forward troops encouraging them when the leading English mounted patrols were seen just after crossing the Bannockburn. Recognising the Scottish king by the gold coronet he was wearing, one of the English knights, Sir Henry de Bohun, set his lance and charged. But Bruce skillfully avoided the deadly point and, rising in his stirrups, cleft de Bohun's helmet and skull with his battleaxe. On being reproached by his generals for the risk he had taken, it is said that he merely remarked: 'Alas I have broken my good battleaxe.'

King Edward was relying on the pomp and chivalry of his large host over-awing the Scots whom at last he had drawn into a set-piece confrontation. But the Scotsmen stood calmly and firmly as the mass of galloping horses bore down on them. The horses pulled up and shied off in front of the serried ranks of spears. The Scots counter-attacked, driving the English from the field — at the cost of only one Scotsman killed.

With English morale low, Edward decided to end the fighting for the day and move his army to new and stronger positions nearer Stirling. Bruce and his commanders watched this vast English army moving away in the distance and crossing the Bannockburn. The disparity in numbers was so great that Bruce was advised to withdraw westwards to carry on guerrilla warfare. Then Sir Alexander Seton, who had been leading a Scots contingent in the English army, defected to Bruce's headquarters and described the miserable plight of the English in the Carse and their low morale. 'Now's the time and now's the hour,' he cried, 'and Scotland shall be free!'

Bruce knew he now had his enemy where he had always want-

K Robert (9)
Bruce and his
second wyff
dochter to the

ed him — where he could not manoeuvre or use his cavalry effectively. He would attack after first light on the following day.

The 24th June broke fine and sunny, and the Scots, after an early meal, moved down to the plain. Mass had been celebrated, for it was St John's Day, and when they came to within some hundreds of yards of the English, they again knelt for a few moments in prayer. Edward, seeing the Scots kneel, is reported to have called out: 'Ha! They kneel for mercy!'

'Yea, sire,' said one of his staff, 'they kneel for mercy, but not from you. These men mean to attack.'

At that moment the English trumpets sounded the alarm and the cavalry rushed to saddle up, don their armour and surcoats and make ready. The Earl of Gloucester, who led the English main body, at once ordered it to charge. He had not time to don his surcoat, with his glittering crests, and, unrecognised, fell dead on the Scottish spears and the charge was halted much as Clifford's had been by Moray the day before. Both sides now became locked together so that archer support was impossible. The English vanguard broke — and its wounded and riderless horses, careering back upon the main body, threw it into confusion.

The English archers tried to reform but the inferior Scottish cavalry rode them down. Jubilant Bruce now saw brought his own strong reserve division into the fight. Turning to his commander Angus Og, he exclaimed: 'My hope is constant in thee' — and the Islesmen rushed upon their foes. The English line began to give.

Edward II, sensing the day was lost, was at last persuaded by his own commanders to retreat to Stirling Castle. Having seen his king safely on the way, Sir Giles d'Argentine is reported as saying: 'Sire, your reign was committed to me; you are now in safety. There is your castle, where your person can be in safety. I have not been accustomed to flee, and I will continue no further — I bid you adieu.' With that, he returned to the battle and charged straight into the Scots. So perished Sir Giles, famed at the time as the bravest knight in all Christendom.

When the royal standard was seen leaving the field, the whole army began to waver. At this juncture, whether on Bruce's orders or from sheer exuberance, the 'small folk' abandoned their reserve position and came rushing down the escarpment on to the plain to join the battle. At the sight of what they took to be further Scottish reserves, the whole English army disintegrated and fled, pursued in every direction. A party of Scots horsemen followed King Edward towards the castle, one man reportedly seized the royal rein. But the stout escort of knights beat him off and the King escaped capture.

The centre of the English army fled to the Forth and to destruction, while the luckless left flank were forced back into the muddy gorge of the Bannockburn at high tide, where the most of them perished. In the words of contemporary chroniclers: 'Bannockburn betwixt the braes was so charged with horses and men that men might pass dry over it upon drowned horses and men.'

The guards left with the English supply train were massacred after the battle and the spoils captured were enormous. The English casualties were very heavy, nearly all the foot and archers being killed or captured, while contemporary records give 700 of the cavalry as dead, including many nobles and knights. Many other nobles were taken prisoner and were later held to ransom. The Scottish casualties are not known, but must have been considerable.

Bruce himself seems to have rated the charge of Angus Og's clansmen as of the highest importance in the battle, for the MacDonalds claimed the honour of always being the 'Right of Line' in royal armies and he gave into Angus's domain many valuable lands and islands in the west. The king's exclamation to him at the crisis of the battle is preserved today in the Clan Ranald motto.

And what of Edward II? Sir Philip Moubray rightly refused the king entry to Stirling Castle as this would have meant his certain capture. With a small but devoted escort and pursued all the way, Edward escaped to Dunbar where he secured a small rowing boat which took him to Berwick. It was an ignominious end to his campaign to conquer Scotland, which had begun with his boastful resolution to wipe out 'Robert de Brus who calls himself King of Scotland'.

King Robert the Bruce proved himself at Bannockburn to be not only a superb leader of men but also a very great general. His place as a great national hero is assured for all time. By the Battle of Bannockburn, Scotland became again a free and independent country. It was the greatest victory that the Scots ever gained, although it took some years before the English, in the Declaration of Arbroath (1320) and then the Treaty of Northampton (1328), gave formal recognition of the results achieved — by acknowledging Bruce as an independent monarch and formally renouncing English overlordship of Scotland. Bannockburn had certainly made Scotsmen feel, more than ever they had done before and possibly since, that they were one people and one nation.

As so often in Scottish history, the benefits of a great achievement or a mighty victory were soon dissipated. Bruce died in June 1329, aged 53. In 1331 his son David, aged just six years old, was crowned king. Bruce's nephew Thomas Randolph became regent before dying a year later. But trouble was brewing. In 1332, urged on by Edward III of England, a number of Scottish nobles, who had been deprived of their lands for siding with the English against Bruce, landed in Fife. Edward took Berwick in 1333. Seeing the way things were going, large numbers of Scottish nobles and clergy changed sides, with the result that the Lowlands of Scotland were easily overrun and garrisoned by the English who filled them with their own merchants, clergy and settlers.

In this turbulent period, the 10-year old king David and his child wife were sent to France for safety. The regency was entrusted to Bruce's 17-year old grandson Robert Stewart who put up a valiant fight. He drove the English garrison out of Bute and in 1339, with the help of a French expeditionary force, captured Perth. In 1340, he had cleared Scotland north of the Forth. Finally, in 1341, he was able to bring his young uncle David back from France and hand over to him the government of the country.

The English were by now fully engaged in France with the Hundred Years War. This gave the Scots a badly needed respite. Stirling and Edinburgh were recaptured, but in 1346 David was taken prisoner by the English after rallying to help out the French army. There followed 12 years in England — which David found an easier life than the burdens of kingship in Scotland. Robert Stewart once more became regent, and following David's death in 1371 took the throne as Robert II, the first Stewart king. He died in 1390 after an unremarkable reign and was succeeded by his son Robert III, who in turn quickly abdicated when he learned he was expected to fight off invaders!

Right: *1929-vintage statue of Robert the Bruce alongside the entrance to Edinburgh Castle.*

This then was the pattern of Scotland's misrule — as all the benefits of Robert the Bruce's victories were wasted. The reasons were clear, however. Of the eight kings who followed the Bruce, only the two Roberts had been adults. David II was five, James I was twelve, James II was six, James III was ten, James IV was fifteen, and James V was just over one year of age — so that for decades Scotland was ruled by regents. Among these royal novices, it was the young James IV who was to be immortalised — following the infamous Battle of Flodden.

Relations between England and Scotland had already rapidly deteriorated following Henry VIII's succession to the English throne. And so James was only too willing to answer the French queen's plea for support against the English following Henry's attack on France in 1512. James sent word that if Henry did not withdraw from France then he, himself, must invade England. His message was ignored.

Thus, with perhaps the biggest Scottish army ever assembled, James crossed the border, captured key English strongholds and awaited the oncoming English army. As the armies came into sight of each other on 9 September 1513, James committed the deadly error of allowing his enemy to place themselves between the Scots and their road back to Scotland. His final error was to order his men to leave their position upon Flodden Hill and toil over marshland to attack the English.

The English foot soldiers were better armed, their 'bills' (short spears with axe heads on their shafts) outmatching the Scottish spears. The English were able to close in upon the tight Scottish ranks. The Scots, as ever, defiantly held their ground and were killed where they stood. In the end, the battle became a massacre.

King James IV was himself killed by an arrow in his throat and an axe wound to his head. With him died, too, the flower of Scottish chivalry. Nine earls and 14 lords, the chiefs of many of the great Highland clans, James's natural son Alexander, Archbishop of St Andrews, the Bishop of Caithness, the Bishop of the Isles, the Dean of Glasgow and the Provost of Edinburgh, together with as many as 10,000 of some of Scotland's finest young men, perished that day. Never had their been such a disaster. Hardly a family in Scotland was not mourning the loss of a son or brother or father. Their untimely end is commemorated in the most moving of laments: *The Flowers of the Forest are a' Wede Away.*

The new king, James V, was aged 18 months. Edinburgh's city leaders hastily built the Flodden Wall, expecting further English attack. But the English had suffered heavy losses too, perhaps as many as 6,000 dead, and hadn't the stomach to renew the fight.

By 1541, however, the English were becoming aggressive yet again. Having himself broken with Rome in 1534, their King Henry VIII was set on making Scotland Protestant and so turning her against France. James resisted this. Then, in 1542, James was offered the Crown of Ireland. This gave Henry the pretext he was looking for. Sending his troops across the border, he proclaimed himself Lord-Superior of Scotland. James, already ill and at odds with his nobles, replied by invading England. But his nobles refused to march. On 24 November 1542, James's little army was defeated at Solway Moss. Sick at heart, the Scottish king rode to Falkland. He died shortly after hearing that his wife had given birth to a baby girl. The child was christened Mary and was proclaimed Queen.

SCOTTISH DECLARATION OF INDEPENDENCE

At Bannockburn, the so-called 'small folk' — the ordinary people of Scotland — were determined, as patriots, under Robert the Bruce's great leadership, to defend the independence of their land with their lives. Their spirit was reaffirmed a few years later in 1320, in the immortal words of the Declaration of Arbroath:
'As long as a hundred of us remain alive we will never be subject to English dominion, because it is not for glory or riches or honours that we fight, but for freedom alone, which no worthy man loses except with his life.'

After nearly 30 years of struggle, there is good reason for this great document often being referred to as the Scottish Declaration of Independence.

Above and Right: *This equestrian statue of Robert the Bruce at the site of Bannockburn, just south of Stirling, was unveiled in 1964. His grave is marked in Dunfermline Abbey by a plaque of 1818. His heart is said to be at Melrose Abbey. The story goes that he asked Sir James Douglas to take his heart to Jerusalem. Sir James was killed en route while in Spain and the Bruce's heart was returned to be interred in Scottish soil. Although best known for his military achievements, the Bruce was an enlightened ruler and his reign saw frequent parliaments including the first — in 1326 — to include representatives of both the Scottish nobility and burghs.*

FORTRESS SCOTLAND

Scotland is dotted with castles — ruined or renovated, rugged or just rural retreats for the rich — but Stirling and Edinburgh are the two which are most closely identified with the nation's history. Each castle occupies a secure volcanic outcrop, which has been made even more easily defensible by the scraping of glaciers in the Ice Ages. This same action has in each case left a gentle tail-like ridge at one end of the outcrop, along which a town developed. Both castles were favoured residences of successive Scottish kings, who progressively rebuilt them to become the magnificent structures they are today. Of Edinburgh and its castle we will learn more later. Stirling's importance we know from the previous chapter.

For much of the Middle Ages, the effective capital of the kingdom was wherever the king happened to be in residence. As a result, the town of Stirling, like Edinburgh, shows many of the characteristics of a medieval capital. Both were provided with fine parish churches, which eventually achieved collegiate status. Both also had a magnificent royal abbey of Augustinian canons.

Following his victory at Bannockburn, Robert I (the Bruce) ordered that Stirling Castle should be rendered indefensible, so that it could not be held against him again. However, in the disturbances which followed his death it was once again repaired and occupied by English forces until they were constrained to surrender to Robert the Steward (later to be Robert II) in 1342.

From the later 14th century onwards, there was a great deal of building, and the North Gate of 1381 may be the earliest identifiable building in the castle still to survive. In the course of the 14th and 15th centuries, Stirling provided a prominent backdrop to the continuous turbulence of medieval Scotland. Amongst the best-remembered of such events was the murder by James II within the castle of William, the 8th Earl of Douglas, in 1452, followed by the ejection of his mutilated corpse from a window.

Above: *Scalloway Castle is situated on the southwest coast of the Shetlands' largest island, Mainland. It was built at the end of the 16th century by Patrick Stewart, Earl of Orkney — the Royal Bastard. A cruel despot he ruled the islands with terror and used forced labour to build his castle.*

Left and Above Right: *The House of the Binns, West Lothian. Begun in the 15th century, the house saw remodelling in the 17th and 19th centuries.*

Right: *Dirleton started its life as a Norman earth and timber castle built by the de Vaux family. Extensive 13th century stone building on this site produced a formidable cluster of towers which were added to in succeeding centuries. Besieged and taken by Edward I's troops in 1298 it was retaken by Robert the Bruce. Subsequently it was taken by General Lambton for the Parliamentary forces in 1650 and is today a ruin.*

The esteem in which the castle was held as a royal residence continued to increase throughout the 15th century, and probably reached its climax in the first half of the 16th century during the reigns of James IV and V, both of whom were prodigious builders.

Further events which have earned the castle a place in Scottish folk memory took place in the reign of Mary Queen of Scots — including her coronation within the chapel in 1543, her escape from death by fire in 1561 and the baptism of her son, the future James VI, in 1566.

James VI, who as a baby had been crowned in the parish church at Stirling, had a close connection with the castle throughout his precarious reign, it being the centre of the struggles between rival factions trying to dominate the youthful king.

In 1594 his first son, Prince Henry, was born here, and grandiose schemes for reconstruction were drawn up. Most were abandoned, however, when in 1603 James moved south to accept the English Crown. Despite a promise of regular 'homecomings', the castle entered a twilight phase of royal occupation.

However, Stirling is just one of a chain of romantic castles, most sited in the most gloriously dramatic settings. The builders of these castles had good natural resources, like stone and timber, readily available to them. In an age of seaborne transport and communication, the waters around the islands and sea lochs of Scotland were aids, not barriers, to the establishment and maintenance of maritime lordships and castles.

Proof of the soundness of these building methods is Castle Sween, the oldest standing castle in Scotland, dating from the late 12th century. Situated on a low rocky ridge on the picturesque eastern shore of Loch Sween, Kintyre, both castle and loch take their name form Suibne, progenitor of the MacSween family, rich and powerful Lords of Knapdale and important landowners in Ireland.

Sween Castle is just one of the famed castles of Argyll, which stand like sentries on its deeply indented coastline and are subject to the assaults of the weather of the western seaboard. They conform to the romantic notion that castles are best fitted to a wild, landscape. In fact, inland there is much fertile land which was settled in the Middle Ages, and therefore needed defending. In the Middle Ages, Argyll became a frontier zone between Norwegian dominion over the islands of the west coast, the 'Innse Gall', and the growing power of the kingdom of the Scots on the mainland. But the undisputed sovereignty of the Kings of Scotland over the whole of the western mainland and islands was not finally recognised until the Treaty of Perth (1266), following the Battle of Largs (1263).

Royal works at Tarbert, Skipness and elsewhere show that long after the removal of the Norwegians, the authority of the kings of the Scots still remained precarious, due to the threats of the MacDonald Lords of the Isles. James IV found that declaring the chief of Clan Donald forfeit and getting the other West Highland chiefs to submit to him at Dunstaffnage Castle in 1493 was simply not enough. In the second of two expeditions in the following year he strengthened Tarbert Castle and took control of Dunaverty.

Multi-storey tower houses, lofty, versatile and defensible, became, from the 1400s, the favoured homes for all ranks of landholders for more than three centuries. The west coast towers at Kilchurn, Skipness and Tarbert belong to this classic age of the tower; others of note include Dunollie, Moy, Breachacha and Saddell. Later structures of this style include the rock-island tower of Castle Stalker, a remarkable offshore mid-16th century house of the Stewarts of Appin. But the largest and most distinguished would undoubtedly have been the first Campbell edifice built at Inverary about 1450 and removed in the 18th century.

The great square tower of Drum castle, at Drumoak near Banchory, is one of the three oldest tower houses in Scotland. It was the work of Richard Cementarius, first Provost of Aberdeen and King's master mason, in the late 13th century. In 1323 Robert the Bruce gave the charter of the Royal Forest of Drum to his faithful armour-bearer, William de Irwyn.

Gradually, castles became less fortifications, more homes — sometimes palaces — for the landed gentry of Scotland. The following few are but examples to whet the appetite of any visitor.

The five towers of Fyvie Castle, north-west of Aberdeen, enshrine five centuries of Scottish history, each being named after one of the five families who owned the castle. The oldest part dates from the 13th century and is now probably the grandest example of Scottish baronial architecture.

Set in Morayshire parkland, Brodie Castle is a magnificent edifice. It is old but the family association with the area is even older. The Brodies were endowed with their lands by Malcolm IV in 1160, and a Thane of Brodie is recorded in Alexander III's reign.

House of the Binns, at Linlithgow, West Lothian, is the historic home of the Dalyells, among them General Tam Dalyell who raised the Royal Scots Greys there in 1681. It reflects the early 17th century transition in Scottish architecture from fortified stronghold to more spacious mansion.

The royal palace of Falkland, in Fife, was the country residence of the Stewart kings and queens when they hunted deer and wild boar in the Fife forest. Mary Queen of Scots spent some of the happiest days of her tragic life 'playing the country girl in the woods and parks'. The palace was built between 1501 and 1541 by James IV and James V, replacing the earlier castle and palace dating from the 12th century. The roofed south range contains the Chapel Royal, and the east range the King's bedchamber and the Queens Room (both now restored by the National Trust for Scotland).

Not all castles have survived so perfectly. Dirleton Castle, in East Lothian, is now a cluster of beautiful ruins dating back to 1225, with additions in the 14th and 16th centuries. The castle has had an eventful history, from its first siege by Edward I in 1298 until its destruction in 1650. But despite its ruination, the romantic setting reveals a flavour of a bygone age . . . its garden still encloses a 16th century bowling green surrounded by yew trees.

These are but a few of the castellated treasures Scotland boasts. A more comprehensive list is given at the back of this volume.

Top right: *Skipness Chapel was resited in the castle grounds in the 13th century.*

Right: *An atmospheric detail of Dirleton Castle.*

Far Right: *Skipness Castle is an enclosure castle which was started by Dugald MacSween in the 13th century and was considerably modified over the years. Located on the strategically important northeast coast of Kintyre, it controlled the confluence of Loch Fyne, Kilbrannsn Sound and the Sound of Bute.*

Edinburgh Castle, pride of Scotland.

Left and Right: *Drum Castle — a 13th century great tower over 20m (70ft) tall — was given to Robert the Bruce's armour bearer, William Irvine in the 1320s. The aerial view shows clearly the mansion still owned by the Irvine family, which was built in the first quarter of the 17th century.*

Bottom and Below Right: *Situated on the shores of Loch Awe, Kilchurn Castle is a beautiful ruin. Built in the 15th century by Colin Campbell, it was remodelled by another Campbell — John — in the 1690s to accommodate a private army; it was abandoned in the mid-18th century.*

Below: *Smailholm Tower, near Kelso.*

Above and Left: *Castle Sween stands on the coast of Knapdale on what used to be called Loch Sween. The massive, uncomplicated early design (it was started in the late 11th/early 12th century) has been masked by later medieval additions but its state of preservation is perhaps unsurprising when you consider how thick — over 2m (6.5ft) — the original walls were. It is now a romantic ruin having been slighted during the Civil War.*

Above Right and Below Right: *Falkland Palace, Fife, was built by James IV to the south of an older, 13th century castle, built by James II. James V made major additions and alterations 1537-42, through the services of his architect Sir James Hamilton. The latter had spent some years at the French court, the workmen were all French and the result was a splendid Renaissance façade to delight James's French wife Madelaine, daughter of the powerful French monarch François I.*

Above Left: *Brodie Castle is owned by the family of the same name and stands on land which has been the family's for over 800 years. The castle we see today was built in the 16th and 17th centuries and rebuilt after a fire in 1645. It contains a good art collection.*

Left: *Another view of Kilchurn Castle brooding in early morning mists.*

Above *Fyvie Castle is a spectacular fortified palace. The earliest part dates back to the 14th century — when the Preston Tower was erected. The other tower — the Meldrum — went up in 15th or 16th century and the imposing gatehouse is also late 16th century.*

FROM DAWN OF A CHRISTIAN AGE

Just as the castles of Scotland tell a story of its violent history, forever threatened by attackers and invaders, so the churches and abbeys of Scotland tell of a different type of cultural 'invasion' — Christianity. In this section, we will look at just a few of the great and beautiful buildings that reflect this civilising influence.

When the Romans left this land, they left behind them not only forts, villas and straight roads, they also left Christianity. The new religion was brought to Scotland by the imperial soldiers and administrators, and for the last hundred years of Roman rule, that empire was officially Christian.

Yet it was a Scotsman, born in the Solway area but educated in Rome, who must be given the credit for introducing Christianity to his homeland. This little-known 4th century missionary, St Ninian, preceded the more celebrated St Columba and St Augustine by almost 200 years. The gospel was first been introduced by St Ninian in AD 397 at Whithorn, where he established his stone church 'Candida Casa'. From there his followers spread the Word through the country.

The island of Iona, however, is more usually credited with being the launch point of Christianity in Scotland. The tiny 1,800-acre west coast isle has a special significance for all Christians because that is where, in AD 563, Columba and his followers arrived from Ireland to extend the religion in Scotland and the north of England. An abbey, other sacred buildings and historic sites are visited by pilgrims from all over the world.

In this section, we will look at only a smattering of religious sites in a journey from Columba's west to the gentler Borders. Columba and his followers took the same journey in their mission to spread their Gospel. Indeed, as we shall learn from the accompanying panel about beautiful Loch Ness, his journey was not without drama.

It is, however, to the south that we now journey — to see a very different Scotland, one which most graphically shows how both the warlike and peaceloving aspects of this country's history have left their marks side by side. For in the beautiful Scottish Borders, alongside the ruins of battered castles and forts, stand examples of Christian architecture at its most perfect.

Hidden in this forgotten country nestling in Scotland's south-eastern corner, between England and Edinburgh, is a land of great contrasts and surprises. Contrasts between soft fields and rugged shoreline, and between splendour and ruin. High hills and moors bound the region on three sides, the North Sea on the other. Through its lush river valleys the great waters of the Tweed, Teviot, Yarrow and Ettrick flow. Almost half the region's 1,800 square miles are more than 305m (1,000ft) high.

Below: *King David I (1124-53) founded Melrose Abbey, now ruined but hauntingly beautiful.*

Above Right: *Detail of the ceiling of Iona Abbey.*

Below Right: *Dryburgh Abbey burial place of Sir Walter Scott..*

The Scottish Borders greatly prizes its peaceful way of life. It was, after all, hard won. As history records, before the area could establish its own identity and way of life, it had to fight off the advances of first the Romans and then the English. In between, there were numerous internal scores to settle. It was a struggle that was to continue unbroken for almost seven centuries, through the wars of independence and the time of the Border Reivers. While much of the Borders was inevitably destroyed in the course of these tumultuous times, happily much remains today to tell the tale.

Traces of camps and hill forts survive from the days when Celt, Pict, Scot and Saxon did battle with one another. Tower houses — like 16th century Aikwood Tower in the Ettrick Valley — that held out the English border raiders stand proudly and defiantly on commanding hilltop sites.

Less blemished by time and conflict is Traquair, said to be the oldest inhabited house in Scotland. It has colourful historical associations with Mary Queen of Scots and the Jacobite risings.

Four of Scotland's greatest historical prizes lie in these lands, together representing the greatest concentration of medieval religious houses in Scotland. With a medieval majesty that still manages to shine through the spoiling and the dereliction they have suffered, the great Border abbeys of Jedburgh, Kelso, Melrose and Dryburgh stand testament to the past. Their story is perhaps best told through the ruins of the proud Abbey of Melrose . . .

A little to the east of the town, beside the winding River Tweed, is a secluded spot called Old Melrose. It is here that Melrose's story begins with the arrival of Celtic monks deep in the Dark Ages, shortly before the year 650. It was at this time that St Aidan of Lindisfarne established a monastery, 'Mailros', bringing monks from the Columban monastery on Iona. Mailros then lay within the Anglian kingdom of Northumbria, and its first abbot, Eata, was one of 12 Saxon youths taught by Aidan. The first prior, St Boisil, a quiet and unassuming monk, gave his name to the local village of St Boswells.

The abbey's story continues with the advent of the Cistercians in 1136, who through their diligence and hard work created one of the richest and most magnificent buildings in Scotland. The abbey church of Melrose is one of the finest expressions of 'the architecture of solitude' practised by the Cistercians. Much of the rose-coloured ruin visitors see today dates from a rebuilding of the war-damaged monastery in the late 14th and 15th centuries, by which date the austere architecture for which the Cistercians were famed, had given way to a far more ornate style.

Melrose Abbey has close associations with many famous historical figures, among them St Aidan, St Cuthbert and St Waltheof, King David I and King Robert the Bruce of Scotland and King Richard II of England.

The historian the Venerable Bede, in his *Life of Saint Cuthbert*, wrote of the great missionary's visit to the abbey: 'Now he [St Cuthbert] entered first the monastery of Melrose which is enclosed for the most part by a loop of the River Tweed, and which was then ruled by its abbot, Eata, the most meek and simple of all men.'

Within a radius of just a few miles are the splendid ruins of the three other great Border abbeys: Kelso, Jedburgh and Dryburgh.

Kelso Abbey, even in its fragmentary state, is a great piece of architecture. What can still be seen today is the west end of the great abbey church of the Tironseians, brought to Kelso in 1128 by King David I to demonstrate that his control stretched right down to the English border.

Jedburgh Abbey is in a more complete state. Also founded by David I, around 1138, it is memorable chiefly as a dramatically sited ruin viewed soon after a traveller's arrival from England. Its position, however, meant that it was the target of raids by more belligerent visitors from across the border, becoming devastated in the 16th century.

Dryburgh Abbey, remarkably complete, is situated beside a most picturesque stretch of the River Tweed. Here, on a sheltered tongue of lush ground, the White Canons of the Premonstratensian Order established their first home on Scottish soil in 1150. Though the monastery never quite aspired to the heights of wealth and political influence enjoyed by its neighbouring three abbeys, it proved nonetheless their equal as a source of attraction to the many English raiding parties that bedevilled Border life for some three centuries. The monastery never recovered from the ravages of English armies in the 1540s. Today, Dryburgh is perhaps best remembered as the burial place of poet and novelist Sir Walter Scott.

Scott wrote: 'Who knows not Melville's beechy grove and Roslin's rocky glen. Dalkeith, which all the virtues love, and classic Horthenden.'

He was talking about the architectural treasures — like 15th century Rosslyn Chapel, one of Scotland's outstanding works of Gothic architecture — of Midlothian, the region sandwiched between the Borders country and Scotland's capital, Edinburgh.

Midlothian and the Borders, by virtue of their strategic position, have been at the heart of Scottish drama and culture over the centuries, and a sense of history everywhere surrounds one. They boast a rich heritage of prehistoric earth dwellings, ancient monuments, hill forts, picturesque churches, historic houses and dramatic castles like Borthwick and Crichton, famed in literature. But their green and tranquil valleys were once the scenes of clashes of arms between feudal lords and, later, between rival monarchs. And perhaps the most famed of these was the amazing lady who held an entire nation in thrall . . . Mary Queen of Scots. It was due to her disputed claim to the throne of England that so many churches and the four beautiful Borders abbeys were reduced to ruins, as we shall see in the following chapter.

Above and Right: *Urquhart Castle stands on the shores of Loch Ness. While today's ruins date back to the 12th century we know that the site has been in continuous occupation for 2,000 years and was visited by St Columba in AD 465.*

NESSIE

More than 200 million years ago, a great movement of the Earth's crust created the Great Glen, a 96km (60 miles) long cleft cutting diagonally across the heart of Scotland. Twenty thousand years ago glaciers scoured and smoothed the glen, creating four great lochs along its length: Linnhe, Lochy, Oich and Ness. Loch Ness is by far the largest — nearly 40km (25 miles) long and only about 3km (2 miles) at its widest point. From the air, Loch Ness looks like a giant 'slash' across the map of Scotland. The lake is more than 300m (1,000ft) deep, with waters blackened by the peat-stained rivers that flow into it.

In recent years, new roads were built along the bank of Loch Ness, opening up the Great Glen, and visitors to the magnificent area 'discovered' the now-famous Loch Ness Monster. But how could a supposedly prehistoric beast, whose ancestors must have lived in the lake for thousands of years, have remained hidden for so long? The truth, of course, is that the existence of this creature from the deep had been recognised by the local Scots for centuries.

The first recorded sighting of Nessie, as it has become affectionately known, was as far back as the birth of Christianity in these northern reaches. It was made by no less than a personage than Saint Columba himself.

The saint travelled from his home in Celtic Dalriada, west Scotland, to the Great Glen in AD 465 converting the heathen Picts to Christianity. During the course of this trip, Columba called at the home in Glen Urquhart of a noble named Emchath and converted him and his household. The discovery a fragment of a brooch recently revealed that this Pictish home was probably a location that has since enthralled visitors as being one of the most dramatic vistas in Scotland: the site of Urquhart Castle, which sits on a rocky promontory jutting into Loch Ness. Although the earliest record of the castle is from the 13th century, it is now clear that the site has been occupied for 2,000 years.

During his mission to Loch Ness, Columba found the locals recovering the body of a neighbour who had been attacked by a beast of the depths while out swimming. One of the saint's followers swam out into the loch to retrieve a boat when he, too, was confronted by the creature.

According to St Columba's biographer Adomnan, abbot of Iona: 'A strange beast rose from the water something like a frog, except that it was not a frog.' Columba ordered the monster: 'Go no further, nor touch that man.' At which the wild predator sank meekly back into the deep.

That was the beginning of the legend of the Loch Ness monster. It is a legend that has been kept alive over the centuries through Scottish folklore, which tells of kelpies (malignant water sprites) disguising themselves as horses to lure and kill human victims. Locals have always referred to their mysterious neighbour as a 'water horse' rather than a monster. Children were warned not to swim in Loch Ness because of the giant kelpie. In Gaelic, the creature was known as *Niseag*.

It was only in the 1930s, when a new road was being cut into the rocky north shore of the lake, that outsiders began to take notice of Nessie. Now monster hunting has become a minor industry, with underwater cameras, echo sounders and even miniature submarines plumbing the depths — but nevertheless failing to find conclusive proof of Nessie's existence. The loch presents investigators with problems. It can play tricks on the eyes. Its high shorelines cast deep shadows and reflections. It is sometimes completely calm in a way that the sea rarely is, and ripples in the water can appear exaggerated. Sceptics have attempted to explain away many mysterious sightings of unidentified creatures as being the result of boats' wakes or wind changes or simply logs in the water.

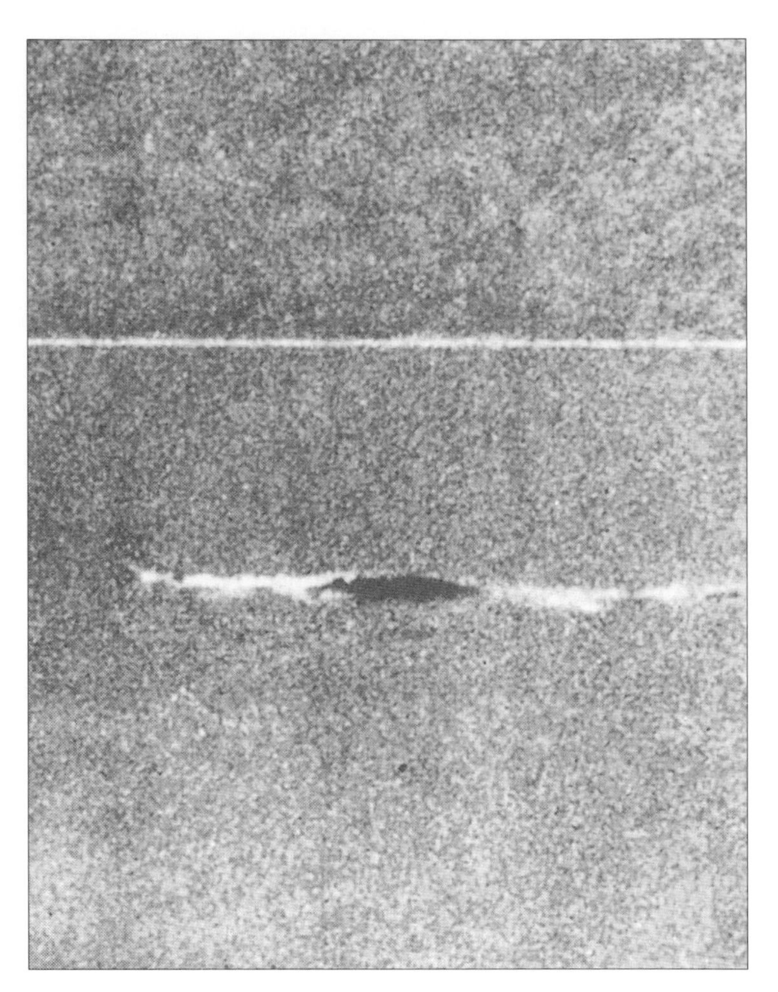

However, one of the world's most respected naturalists, the late Sir Peter Scott, who helped launch the Loch Ness Phenomena Investigation Bureau, was sufficiently impressed with research to announce: 'I believe there are between 20 and 50 creatures down there — and I believe they are related to the plesiosaurs.'

Since the plesiosaur is long extinct, Scott's theory means that the creatures in Loch Ness must have been cut off from the sea at the end of the last Ice Age. That makes Nessie and her ancestors up to 70 million years old!

If Nessie exists, why have no bodies or bones ever been found on the shoreline? Scientists say that water pressure in the great depths slows down decomposition and allows time for eels to dispose of the remains of any defunct monsters. And so cold is it that bodies of drowned men — never mind monsters — seldom return to the surface.

Above: *It's hard to believe that Nessie exists but when such experts as Sir Peter Scott don't rule it out, indeed are enthusiastic, you begin to wonder . . .*

Right: *Urquhart Castle stands on a promontory jutting into the peat-blackened waters of Loch Ness. It was here, perhaps, that St Columba met Emchath. This moody castle has a long history. It changed hands many times between English and Scot during the wars of the 13th and14th century. In 1313 it became the property of one of Robert the Bruce's counsellors, Randolph Earl of Moray.*

Above: *Another abbey founded by David I, Kelso was one of the most spectacular Romanesque abbeys in Britain. Particularly wealthy — by 1300 it controlled the revenues from some 40 churches.*

Right: *The ruins of Melrose Abbey in the lush hills of the Borders east of Galashiels. Probably founded by St Aidan in the 7th century, David I invited the Cistercians to establish the medieval abbey. The ruins we can see today date back to the 14th and 15th century; the abbey stood close to the road used by invading English armies and so was frequently damaged and rebuilt.*

The ruins of Melrose Abbey.

Left and Below: *Kelso Abbey.*

Right and Below Right: *Melrose Abbey.*

What caused the deterioration and decay of such wealthy foundations? War certainly played its part: the Borders' abbeys resounded to the brute noise of war regularly, but neglect was probably the main culprit. Following the Reformation when the fixtures and fittings were removed, with windows and roof lead gone stone robbing — a time honoured practice the world over — took hold. Many a local farm or country house would have accepted gleefully the cheap, fine quality stone available for reuse! The most vandalised Scottish abbey of them all was that of Scone which was so destroyed by a mob, following John Knox's tirade against idolatry in 1559, that it is not even listed as an ancient monument because too little remains.

Today, as with the great English medieval foundations at Jervaulx, Rievaulx and Fountains, all that remains are beautiful skeletons which still seem to retain a fragmentary feeling of quiet, reflective solitude.

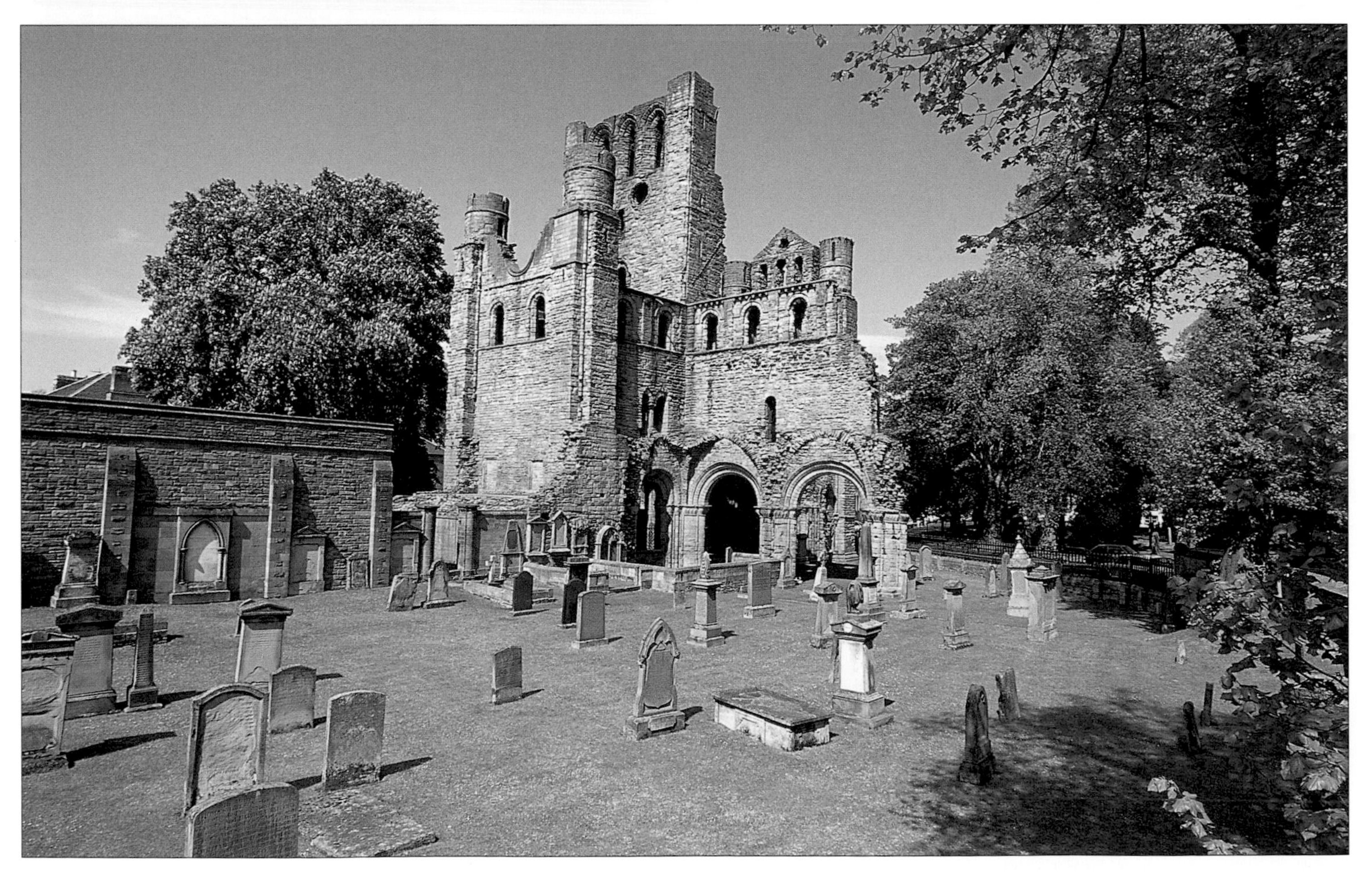

Above and Left: *Melrose Abbey. The beautiful detail of the window exemplifies the style of Gothic architecture called 'Decorated' which can be described as 'more tracery than glass'.*

Right: *Dryburgh Abbey ceiling detail.*

Left, Below Left and Right: *Dominating the Jed River, Jedburgh Abbey was founded in 1138 as a priory of the Augustinian canons.*

Below: *The Cross of St John outside Iona Abbey.*

Below Right: *It was to Iona that St Columba came by coracle from Ireland in AD 563 to spread the Word. The island is just off the west coast of Mull, separated by the Sound of Iona, which is just over 1km (0.75 miles) wide. The island has a long religious history: used by the druids before the birth of Christ, under St Columba it became the centre of European learning.* The Book of Kells *may have been started here (it is preserved today in Dublin); written in Irish with magnificent illustrations it is a manuscript of the four gospels.*

Left: *Iona Abbey and the replica of St John's Cross. St Columba died in AD 597 and Iona settled down to a long period of peace which was shattered by roving Norsemen in 795, 801, 806 — when 68 monks were massacred at Martyrs' Bay — 825 and finally 986 when the abbot and 15 monks were killed. The monastery was rebuilt in 1074 and in 1430 the Bishopric of the Isles was formed. Iona became a cathedral in 1500, but the reformation was just around the corner and all the religious buildings were broken up and most of the crosses on the island defaced. It would not be until 1910 that the abbey was restored.*

Bottom: *The burial ground on Iona — it was recorded in 1549 that 60 kings of Scotland and Norway were buried here.*

Right: *Iona Beach.*

Below: *Iona Abbey detail.*

MARY QUEEN OF SCOTS

Few other figures in Scottish history are as well known as Mary Queen of Scots, who lived from 1542 to 1587. Her reign in Scotland lasted only seven years, yet she played her part in a drama which still fascinates historians and visitors alike. She had in full measure the strange charm of the Stewart (the spelling was later changed to Stuart) dynasty which so often added turbulence and uncertainty to Scotland's story. But this queen's life was part of a larger drama, played out in the royal houses of Scotland, France and England.

Mary was born at a troubled time for Scotland, which was experiencing the first upheavals of the Reformation. The Protestant reformers favoured an alliance with England, as King Henry VIII of England was a vigorous opponent of Catholicism. Meanwhile the supporters of Catholicism looked towards France.

Mary's grandmother was Henry's sister, Margaret Tudor. But Mary's mother, Mary of Guise, was of the French royal house. Her husband, King James V, died at Falkland Palace only a week after Mary was born at Linlithgow Palace. With the religious struggle intensifying between France and England, France expected Scotland (with its Catholic monarchy) to side with it against the English King Henry. Thus Scotland was drawn into an English-French quarrel — a dangerously unstable political situation for the young queen.

Just before her birth, a half-hearted attempt by Scotland to aid France had ended in defeat by England at Solway Moss. Soon King Henry VIII was well aware that several Scottish lords were unhappy with the established church and demanded that the infant Mary should marry his own son Edward, thus creating a Protestant dynasty on both sides of the border. Before Mary was three years old, Henry had sent an army to back his claim in an episode known as the 'rough wooing'.

The English armies destroyed the Border abbeys, and burned the palace of Hollyroodhouse in Edinburgh and many other parts of southern Scotland. By the time Mary was five years old, even though King Henry VIII had died, English forces under Edward VI defeated the Scots at the Battle of Pinkie, near Musselburgh, in September 1547 and occupied their country.

Many Scots did not know which way to turn. Though the tide of anti-Catholicism was gradually rising, the English invaders, representing the new Protestantism, were unpopular. In the absence of a strong monarch, the nation was indecisive — then finally appealed to France to rid the country of the English invaders. Already a pawn in a political game, the price for this was the removal of the future queen to France. At the age of only six, amid much conflict and bloodshed, Mary sailed from Dumbarton Castle in 1548.

She returned to Scotland at the age of 18, already widowed following the death of the king of France. Contemporary accounts speak of her beauty: she was tall, dark-eyed and graceful.

Although the new Protestant religion had by no means claimed all influential Scots, by the time of Mary's return reformers like John Knox were already preaching armed resistance to any attempt by the monarch to interfere with their style of worship. However, Mary had particular support in the Highlands, which were still mainly Catholic.

Above: *Wooden ceiling panel in Mary Queen of Scots' outer chamber at the Palace of Holyroodhouse. Poor Mary spent much of her life in confinement: from her sojourn aged three on the Isle of Inchmahome to keep away from Henry VIII's 'rough wooing', a year in the castle of Loch Leven where she was forced to abdicate her crown and then 19 years in the hands of English Queen Elizabeth I until the Babington Plot led to her execution at Fotheringay in 1587.*

Right: *Mary's bedroom in Holyroodhouse Palace.*

Mary fell in love with Henry, Lord Darnley, whom she described as 'the lustiest and best-proportioned lang man' that she had ever met (he was over six feet tall). They were married in 1564 in the Chapel Royal at Holyrood. He soon proved to be arrogant, impetuous, fond of taverns and thoroughly unreliable. Mary thereafter excluded him from court business. He also became jealous of her secretary and close friend, Italian musician David Rizzio. As part of a wider power-plot, Rizzio was murdered by Darnley and his supporting conspirators before the queen's eyes in the Palace of Hollyroodhouse.

Shortly after, Mary gave birth to a son, destined to be James VI

of Scotland — later James I of England, after the childless English Queen Elizabeth. Factions and plots among Scotland's noble families were rife at this time, in a complex political situation involving the church and state. It was rumoured that Mary was to be removed from the throne and Darnley set up as regent over her child.

By 1567, the year after the birth of her child, Mary had pardoned the murderers of Rizzio, failed in her attempt to reconcile Darnley and had become attracted to one of her staunch supporters, the Earl of Bothwell. Then Darnley was found murdered after a mysterious explosion at the Kirk o' Field, Edinburgh. Bothwell was implicated but soon had himself acquitted of the accusations.

The Earl of Bothwell abducted Mary and took her, perhaps willingly, to Dunbar Castle. Scotland was shocked and rebellion loomed when it became known that they had married. Besieged on their honeymoon in Borthwick Castle, Midlothian, both Bothwell and Mary escaped and raised an army. Their forces assembled at the Palace of Seaton, in East Lothian. They were challenged by an army of confederate lords at Carberry Hill, southeast of Edinburgh, where they were defeated on 15 June 1567. Bothwell slipped away (he eventually ended his days in prison in Denmark) while Mary was taken captive. After being led in an unseemly short red petticoat through the jeering crowds of Edinburgh, the deposed queen, still only 24, was imprisoned in Loch Leven Castle.

Loch Leven Castle will forever be associated in the memory of Mary Queen of Scots. She had been a frequent visitor during her short, tragic reign, perhaps because it was a marvellous place from where she could enjoy her favourite sport of hawking. She probably visited first within months of her return from France in 1561. Two years later she debated long and hard with John Knox in the castle's great hall as to whether Roman Catholics should be persecuted or tolerated. In 1565 Mary, with her second husband Lord Darnley, dined at Loch Leven.

But within two days of her defeat at the battle of Carberry Hill she was a prisoner at the island castle which had given her so much pleasure. Her jailer was Sir William Douglas, Laird of Loch Leven and a die-hard rebel. 'Guard was continually kept at the castle day and night, except during supper, at which time the gate was locked with a key,' wrote Giovanni Correr, Venetian Ambassador to France, reporting in May 1568 on Mary's imprisonment.

Loch Leven Castle, whose surviving buildings are outstanding, is among the most important medieval monuments in Scotland. Indeed, the lofty tower house on the island which was Mary's prison for much of her stay has a claim to be among the oldest in the country, and parts of the courtyard may well perpetuate defences erected as early as 1300.

Mary, who miscarried twins within a month of her arrival, was housed in the third floor of the tower house. Because of her state of health, she was allowed a doctor, in addition to two ladies-in-waiting and a cook. She occupied her time during captivity in needlework and walking in the castle grounds.

The most momentous event during her imprisonment occurred in June 1567 when she was forced to abdicate in favour of her infant son, christened Charles James. He succeeded to the throne as James VI and was crowned at Stirling five days later. The Laird of Loch Leven had the castle's guns fired and bonfires lit in the courtyard to celebrate the event. The recently deposed Queen was not amused.

The castle walls held Mary for less than a year. In May 1568, with the help of boatman Willie Douglas, she escaped across the loch. She fled to the west, rallying supporters as she went. Yet within a matter of days of her escape her army was decisively defeated by Protestant forces (often known as the Lords of the Congregation) at Langside, near Glasgow. She fled southwards and her last night in Scotland was spent at Dundrennan Abbey, in Galloway.

Mary, former Queen of Scots, went into England, and in May 1568 threw herself on the mercies of the Queen of England, her cousin Elizabeth. Not forgetting Mary's long-standing claim to the English, as well as Scottish, throne, Elizabeth promptly imprisoned her once more. Without ever seeing Scotland again, Mary remained in captivity south of the border, a pawn in the political game played around her, for 19 long years.

Above: *Dumbarton Castle, nestling below Dumbarton rock, volcanic basalt, jutting into the Clyde.*

Below Left and Right: *Loch Leven Castle will always be remembered for its associations with Mary Queen of Scots who spent nearly a year in unhappy captivity within its cramped confines. For it is a small structure with spartan facilities — very different from her usual quarters in Holyroodhouse. The keep was started in the 14th century; the walls and drum tower were 16th century additions. Entrance was by means of a ladder to the second floor of the five-storey keep. As can be seen from the photograph* (**Right**) *the brickwork is immaculate although the interior of the keep is gutted.*

Despite many calls for her execution as a traitor, Elizabeth refused to send her to the block, until a plot — the so-called Babington Plot — was uncovered to assassinate the English queen and replace her with Mary who would bring back Catholicism to England. Mary was found guilty of complicity and, four months later, was led to the block at Fotheringhay Castle, Northamptonshire. Before some 300 spectators, she calmly walked to her death dressed in black on 8 February 1587. Her outer clothes were removed, revealing a dark red petticoat and bodice, the colour of blood and the Catholic church's colour of martyrdom. Before the axe fell, Scotland's most romantic queen forgave her executioners, saying: 'I hope you shall make an end of all my troubles.'

Below and Right: *Dumbarton Castle was the capital of the ancient Kingdom of the Britons of Strathclyde until it merged again into the Kingdom of Scotland in about 1018. It was also used by the Hanoverian kings as one of the garrison points to control Scotland. Without doubt it can lay lay claim to being the strongpoint with the longest recorded history in Scotland.*

CLANS, WITCHES AND GIANTS

In Gaelic, the word 'clann' means family or children. The peculiarly Scottish social system of clans was a distinctly Gaelic tribal culture — but one which eventually encompassed many peoples of different ancient origins, whether Celtic, Norse or Norman-French. By the 13th century, the clan system was well-established in the Highlands of Scotland. And in its 15th century heyday, it even threatened the authority of the monarchy.

The geography of the Highlands and Islands may, in the distant past, have played a part in the formation of the clans as social groups, each on its own territory, divorced from its neighbours. And the clans were completely separated by language, custom and geography from the southern 'Sassunachs' (nowadays spelled 'Sassenachs' — meaning of Saxon origin, a word applicable both to the English and to Lowland Scots).

Though increasingly brought into contact with the rest of Scotland, the clan system survived intact until, as we shall see, it was partly dismantled following the Jacobite uprising which ended at Culloden in 1746. Nevertheless, the tribal pride in belonging to a clan lives on to this day and is still a vital part of the richness of cultural life in Scotland. Indeed, with the migrations of Scots in recent centuries, the clans have spread their individual identities throughout the world.

The clan was basically a tribe. At its head was the chief, who was also the owner of its lands. A large clan might have branches or septs, headed by chieftains who originally would be related to, or appointed by, the chief. Not all members of a clan were related, for outsiders could be accepted. When the clan system was at its height, when it had least contact with 'Lowland ways', it was common practice for the sons of the clan chief to be 'boarded out' to other families living nearby.

Growing up with other members of this extended family helped to bond the clan unit together and to foster allegiance. Thus the chief was a kind of tribal father to whom both lesser chieftains and ordinary clansmen gave their loyalty. Such incomers might adopt the name of the chief, but surnames are an unreliable guide to kinship as they were not in general use until relatively late in history. What mattered was loyalty to chief and clan.

The clans lived off the land more-or-less self-sufficiently, with cattle as their main wealth. Stealing cattle (sometimes in order to survive) was widespread, as were territorial disputes between clans. The clansmen did not own land, only the chief, sometimes directly from the crown, sometimes from other superior clan chiefs.

Between the chief and the clansmen were the tacksmen, often related to the chief, by whom they were appointed. They rented from him large tracts of land which they sub-let at rents which allowed them a profit. They were responsible for rent collecting and also for calling out the men of the clan when the chief wanted to go to war. Neither of these duties was particularly popular, and the latter could sometimes involve force if a clansman was unwilling to obey the summons to battle. The system, however, meant that the chief was not personally involved in these operations, and his position as 'father of his people' was unimpaired.

Above: *Dunstaffanage Castle sits on the mouth of Loch Etive where it meets the Firth of Lorn.*

Right: *Ossian's Cave. Ossian was the mythical son of Fingal — builder of the Giant's Causeway. The cave is on the northern side of Aonach Dubh, the last of the 'Three Sisters', on the left as you travel down Glen Coe from Rannoch Moor.*

The clan would normally fight with its chief at its head, the immediate members of his family leading its companies, and each man in the position dictated by his social standing within the clan. The priorities were clear; when one chief, a MacDonell of Keppoch, was asked how much his rents brought him, he replied: 'Five hundred fighting men'.

Not all of a clan chieftain's preoccupations were warlike, however. The most powerful chiefs in some places kept expensive

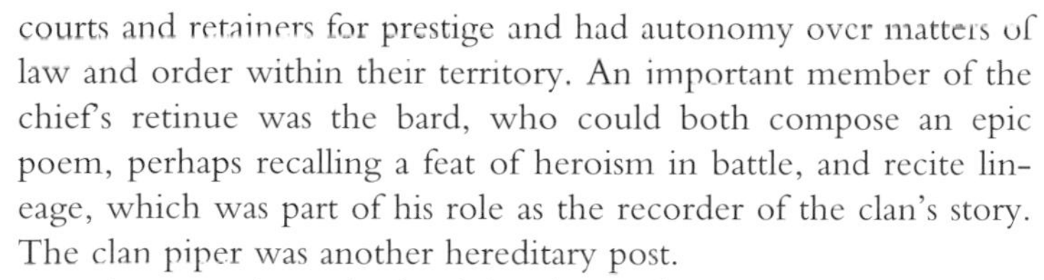

courts and retainers for prestige and had autonomy over matters of law and order within their territory. An important member of the chief's retinue was the bard, who could both compose an epic poem, perhaps recalling a feat of heroism in battle, and recite lineage, which was part of his role as the recorder of the clan's story. The clan piper was another hereditary post.

It is romantic to think of the clan tradition as being mystically Celtic. But it is much more broadly based than that. Some clans have Norman roots and married into Celtic society: Cummings (Comyns), Hays (de la Haye), Frasers (La Frezeliere, ultimately linked to the French 'la fraise', referring to the strawberry shaped device on the family crest), Sinclair (St Clair) and Bruce (Brix, a Normandy place name). Following early Viking raids on Scotland, others have Norse connections: the Macleods of Skye are said to descend from Liot, son of a Norse king; the MacDougalls of Lorne come from the Dougall (Gaelic, 'dark foreigner'), grandson of Norse King Olaf, the Black.

Some clans are linked with ancient monastic houses: the Macnabs ('son of the abbot'); Buchanan ('of the canon's house'); MacTaggart ('son of a priest') and MacPherson ('son of a parson').

Clans with uncertain origins include the MacKenzies who appeared in Ross and Cromarty, claiming descent from their 12th-century kinsman Gilleoin, as do the Mathesons, with lands close to Kyleakin in Wester Ross. The Gunns in Sutherland claim a most unusual descent: they may have been an ancient surviving Pictish tribe, forced into the far north of Scotland.

Clan Donald, the Lords of the Isles, was for generations the most powerful clan in Scotland, especially on the lands by the western seaboard. Great seafarers, the clan controlled the sea lanes with its oared galleys (Gaelic: *birlinn*). Living in semi-royal style, the clan's power brought it into conflict with the crown and the power of Clan Donald was broken before the end of the 15th century.

Mention of the Clan Donald brings us to the best-known, or perhaps most infamous, historical event in clan history. The massacre of Glencoe (the village which sits on Loch Leven at the end of Glen Coe)is a bloody example of the perpetual schisms between individual clans, between the clans and the Lowlanders, between the Catholics and the Protestants, and between Scots and English.

But the history of Glen Coe is much more than the story of a massacre. That event occupied a mere two or three hours in a struggle that went on for at least a thousand years. The whole episode can be seen only in the context of the long and often bitter family rivalries of the Western Highlands. It also gives us an opportunity to gaze upon the grandeur of an area that is one of the world's most celebrated landscapes.

Over the years, hundreds of writers have waxed eloquent in their descriptions of the glen. Perhaps none more than Dorothy Wordsworth when she wrote in her Journal in September 1803: 'The impression was, as we advanced up to the head of the first reach, as if the glen was nothing. Its loneliness and retirement made up no part of my feeling: the mountains were all in all.'

One of the first people to report the wonders of Glen Coe was St Mundus, an Irish disciple of St Columba, who came across from Iona round about the year 600 and settled briefly on a small island in Loch Leven, opposite the mouth of the glen. For centuries this island, Eilaen Munde, the isle of Mundus, was to be the religious centre of the region. But it is not surprising that in a realm as melodramatic, magical and mist-shrouded as this, religion should mix easily with myth and legend.

Glen Coe has produced more than its fair share of giants, monsters and witches. The most famous of the witches was the wicked Corrage who, at her death, was surprisingly offered Christian burial on Eilean Munde. But the waters of Loch Leven erupted in anger and prevented her crossing, so she was buried on the mainland. She returned subsequently to use her storm-raising powers to sink one of the stray ships of the Spanish Armada which was trying to win home by this route. Another well-known witch was Bean Nighe who was occasionally to be seen washing her clothes in the River Coe. Anyone who saw her was doomed to die soon after . . . and it is not surprising to learn that she made an appearance the night before the famous massacre. Amongst the monsters, the most famous was '*Tarb Uisge*', the water bull of Loch Achtriochtan, named after Ossian, who seems to have been one of Scotland's more amiable monsters and did harm to no one.

When it comes to giants, Glen Coe, as befitted its grandeur and the size of its mountains, was the legendary home of one of the greatest Celtic heroes, Fingal. Fingal, or Fionn McCumhail, was the leader of the Feinn tribe and father of the totally mythical Ossian.

Fingal, if he was a historical figure at all, is credited with a defeat of the Vikings in Glen Coe. The first part of this battle took place at Laroch, by Ballachulish, when the Vikings, led by King Erragon of Sora, came up Loch Leven to Inverscaddle Bay with 40 of their ships full of warriors. Most of Fingal's men, the Feinn, were away hunting deer and the crafty Fingal kept the enemy talking until their return. King Erragon suggested that each side should provide their best 140 warriors who would fight it out formally on the field of Achnacon. This suggestion was accepted and the Scots won — but the whole exercise had to be repeated six times, with great blood-

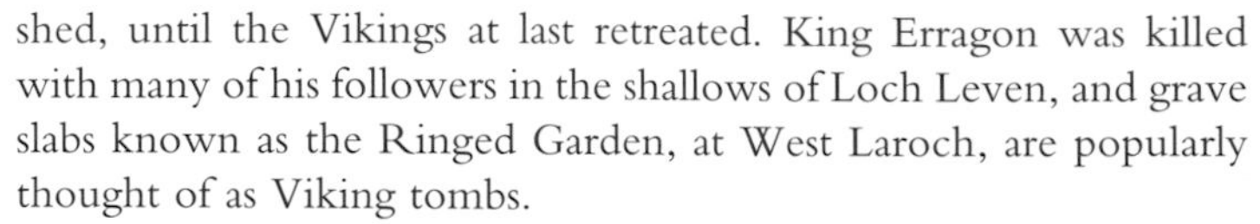

shed, until the Vikings at last retreated. King Erragon was killed with many of his followers in the shallows of Loch Leven, and grave slabs known as the Ringed Garden, at West Laroch, are popularly thought of as Viking tombs.

About the 11th century, Glen Coe passed into the hands of the powerful MacDougall clan, a family of Viking descent, who built up a small empire based at Dunstaffnage Castle, near Oban. In 1308, however, the MacDougall power was shattered when the clan sided with the English against Robert the Bruce. The rival MacDonalds and Campbells fought side by side for Bruce to destroy the MacDougalls at the Battle of the Pass of Brander, 20 miles south of Glen Coe. As part of his reward, Angus Og, chief of the MacDonalds, was given the area by Bruce — and for the next 500 years it was MacDonald country.

THE KILT

The traditional attire of the clansmen was the kilt of tartan. But neither the garments nor the patterns we know today would have been familiar in the ancient Highlands.

The traditional dress was the belted plaid (*plaide* is Gaelic for blanket). This was a rectangle of cloth about 6ft wide, and was held in place by a belt round the waist. The upper part could be arranged in a variety of ways and, the belt having been loosened, it could serve to wrap the wearer in at night.

The modern kilt is simply the lower half of this garment with its pleats stitched.

Credit for its invention is often given to an Englishman, Thomas Rawlinson, who ran an ironworks in Glengarry and Lochaber about 1725. This is not acceptable to all Scots however, and Sir Thomas Innes of Learney, a former Lord Lyon, in his *Tartans of the Clans and Families of Scotland* calls it 'a wretched story' and claims a much longer history.

Right: *Dunstaffanage Castle featured importantly in Scottish history from the days when Alexander II and III used it on their campaigns against the Vikings in the Western Isles; Edward I took it — the Bruce took it back; it was held by the Earls of Argyll and was abandoned in1810. In legend the Stone of Destiny resided here in an ancient building of the Kings of Dalriada until it was removed to Scone by MacAlpin.*

Dunstaffange Castle from the shore of Loch Etive.

MASSACRE OF GLEN COE

The fist hint of trouble in Glen Coe came in the 16th century, when the difference in wealth between the subsistence clans of the remoter Highlands and the more industrious fertile Lowlands began to become more pronounced. In 1501 the Glen Coe MacDonalds, with others, captured the Campbell's island fortress of Innis Chonnell, on Loch Awe, and briefly rescued from his long imprisonment Donald Dhu, the only surviving grandson of the last Lord of the Isles. This was just one of many clashes which occurred over the next 200 years. Glen Lyon, now Campbell country, became a favourite raiding-ground and the scene of many skirmishes. It was to be the ultimate coincidence that a Glen Lyon Campbell captained the Redcoats sent to conduct the massacre.

Some years later, Scottish clans became entangled in the civil war between the English monarchy and the English parliamentarians — in which the MacDonalds backed the royalist Cavaliers whilst the Campbells were the Scottish equivalent of the parliamentary Roundheads. A large MacDonald contingent, including the Glen Coe men under their 11th Chief, fought for the brilliant Marquis of Montrose in his spectacular campaign to save Charles I. It was the Glen Coe men who helped Montrose to find the famous short-cut over the mountains at the Devil's Staircase, east of Glen Coe, which enabled Montrose to attack a much larger Campbell army from the rear, near Fort William. More than 2,000 Campbells were killed and the strategically important town of Inverary was captured by Montrose. After the fall of Montrose, Glen Coe MacDonalds still fought vainly for the Royalist cause.

In 1646 came another famous incident when, on one of the Glen Coe raids into Glen Lyon, the MacDonalds attacked the Clans Menzies and Campbell after a wedding. They killed 36 of them and returned home with great booty.

Decades of cattle-rustling culminated in the so-called Atholl Raid of 1685. Two successive Earls of Argyll had been executed in Edinburgh, and the Campbells were weakened by defeats. The Glen Coe men took advantage of the situation to pillage huge tracts of Campbell territory. The rights and the wrongs of the massacre of Glen Coe, therefore, were less clear cut than folklore and clan rivalry would have us believe.

The massacre was carried out on a branch of the Clan Donald by a regular regiment of the British army, raised from the Clan Campbell. The latter had a long history of anti-Jacobitism and support for the Hanoverian (or otherwise Lowland) government. The Campbell regiment acted under orders from King William III in London who wanted the MacDonalds punished ('extirpated') as part of a government policy designed to bring rebel clans to heel.

The story of the massacre has been told many times. On 27 August 1691 King William offered a pardon to all Highland clans who had fought against him or raided their neighbours, on condition that they took the oath of allegiance before a magistrate by the close of the year. It was a fair enough offer. Old Alastair MacDonald had four months to pluck up courage to make the dread journey to Inverary to obtain pardon for himself and his followers. The alternative was death. Perhaps not taking the threat seriously, Alastair MacDonald left this act of subservience to the last minute, not taking the oath until five days past the deadline. Nevertheless, MacDonald believed that he was safe.

Above: *Looking toward Stob Corrie nan Lochan which can just be seen over the top of the Aonach Dubh.*

Right: *The slopes of Aonach Dubh are reflected in the still waters of Loch Achtriochtan.*

However, a punitive force had already been built up at Fort William and it appeared that the MacDonalds had made enough enemies — King William himself, Secretary of State Sir John Dalrymple of Stair and John Campbell Earl of Breadalbane — to make them seek excuse to regard the oath as invalid. On 1 February 1692 two advance companies were sent to Glencoe under the com-

mand of another man who had a grudge against the MacDonalds: Captain Robert Campbell of Glen Lyon a 60-year old alcoholic and a gambler who had by this time lost anything that the MacDonalds had left of his estates.

Robert Campbell had not received specific orders to attack the MacDonalds when he set out for Glencoe. So, since his niece was married to the Glen Coe chief's younger son, he asked for quarters for his two companies. All were entertained in the homes of the Glen coe MacDonalds most hospitably for 10 days.

On 12 February, Campbell received written orders from Duncanson to kill all MacDonalds under 70 years of age at five o'clock the following morning. It was the way in which Campbell of Glen Lyon turned on his hosts, on his own niece and her husband, in breach of the ultimate ethic of Highland hospitality, which later gave special notoriety to the massacre.

It was mere coincidence that, while he was there as a commissioned officer of King William and acting under direct orders from his superiors, he happened to belong to one of the Campbell families who had suffered most at the hands of the Glen Coe MacDonalds. He was bankrupt and now totally dependent on his army pay. He had very little pride or principle left and was not the sort of person to stand up to his superiors. The other macabre feature of his plight was that, with a force of around 120 men, he was ordered to destroy, in darkness and very poor weather, several hundred people spread over a distance of at least 10 square miles. They expected substantial reinforcements but they were late, perhaps deliberately, leaving all the dirty work to Captain Campbell.

Of the 130-odd officers and men, no more than a dozen bore the surname Campbell. They may have harboured a personal bitterness, but it was not ruthless efficiency which marked the massacre but general incompetence. The force killed only about 10 per cent of the numbers they had been ordered to destroy.

The massacre was merciless enough. At Inverrigan, where Captain Campbell had his quarters, eight or nine MacDonalds were tied up and shot. At Invercoe, one man was shot crossing the river. At Carnoch, where the chief had his house, the old man was shot as he got out of his bed and his wife had her clothes and rings stripped from her. At Achnacon several more were killed, including an old man of 80 and a child. At Achtriochtan, the community where the clan bards used to live, a further group was killed.

In all, about 38 were killed but at least 300 escaped into the hills. By the time reinforcements arrived, there was only one old man left alive in the villages and he was promptly killed. Of those who escaped, many are believed to have died of cold and starvation. Most, survived, including the old chief's two sons — despite specific orders 'to root out the old fox and his cubs'. On the army side, three soldiers were believed killed when they pursued MacDonalds up into the hills. And there was a rumour that two officers had resigned their commissions rather than take part in the massacre.

About two weeks later, news of the massacre began to filter through to London. But it was a piece of investigative journalism by an Irishman, Charles Leslie, which turned Glen Coe into a political scandal. His pamphlet, arguing a high-level cover-up and breach of trust, excited sympathy for many who were not wholly enamoured with Dalrymple as secretary of state, or William of Orange as king. But there were to be no official reprimands for a full three years. Of those responsible for the massacre, Dalrymple had to resign but soon made a political comeback, and Captain Campbell died a pauper in Bruges, Belgium.

The clan system was now slowly heading for collapse — not just in Glen Coe and the western Highlands but throughout the land. Some chiefs were becoming more interested in money than in men, espousing agriculture and forestry, and dispensing with the tacksmen as costly intermediaries. By the 18th century, with agricultural improvements spreading from the Lowlands and with some roadbuilding taking place which made communications easier, clans and their chiefs were brought more and more into contact with 'southern' ways, which subtly eroded their independence and values. The old clan system was gradually being absorbed into a modern economic society

This process of change was noted by Sir Walter Scott in his novel *Rob Roy* where Rob can be seen as a symbol of the old, self-sufficient ways, which contrasted with his distant cousin, Bailie Nicol Jarvie, a Glasgow merchant preoccupied with progress and business. Even so, Rob also acts as a Jacobite agent and sympathiser (as did the real life Rob Roy), demonstrating that, inevitably, the clan system was a part of Scottish politics.

Ultimately, Lowland authority moved against the clans simply because the chiefs could call on loyal fighting men in time of war or rebellion. These 'private armies' were perceived as hotbeds of Jacobitism or at the very least liable to undermine authority.

Of the two MacDonald brothers who escaped the massacre of Glen Coe, John, the 13th Chief of Glen Coe, was formally allowed the king's pardon and rebuilt the family home at Carnoch. His brother Alastair rose for the Jacobite cause in 1715 — and fought alongside John Campbell, son of the captain who had led the massacre. Both men forfeited their estates when their cause was lost.

Thirty years later, Alastair, the 14th Chief of Glen Coe, who had escaped as a baby from the massacre, turned out with his men to fight for Bonnie Prince Charlie and was made a member of the prince's council. The Glen Coe men fought at Culloden . . . and that was truly their last stand. In the miserable period that followed the defeat, their homes were burned once more, their cattle driven away, their clan headquarters at Carnoch destroyed and the chief imprisoned. The chieftainship of the MacDonalds of Glen Coe lost all its meaning. (The title was eventually sold to Lord Strathcona, of the Hudson's Bay Company, Canada.) That year of 1746 also saw the chase in Glen Coe which Robert Louis Stevenson included in his novel *Kidnapped.*

To what would have been a gradual social change by the clans of Scotland, the Battle of Culloden was to give a brutal and bloody impetus.

Right: *Artist's impression of the MacDonalds fleeing for their lives into the snow, chased by English soldiers. Surprisingly few died in battle — 38 out of 300 — but many died from the cold in the aftermath,.*

Above: *The Lost Valley runs between Beinn Fhada and Geàrr Aonach — two of the three sisters of Glen Coe. The arrête at the head of the valley leads to Bidean nam Bean, at 1,150m (3,770ft) the highest mountain in Argyll-shire.*

Left: *Glen Coe during the warmer months.*

Right: *The northern side of Glen Coe is dominated by the Aonach Eagach, a long knife-edged ridgewalk which can be dangerous in extreme conditions. At the Rannoch Moor end of the glen, at the start of the ridge, sits Am Bodach from where this photograph was taken.*

Below Right: *The weather can change very quickly in winter, a cloudless sky can quickly grey over. But the mountains do look spectacular in the snow.*

THE JACOBITE CAUSE

The 17th century was a troubled time both in Scotland and England. James II of England and VII of Scotland was a Roman Catholic, but many whom he ruled were not. His brief reign (1685-88) was marked by unrest and open rebellion in both kingdoms.

By the end of 1688 King James had made himself so unpopular by his despotic methods of government and his attempts to ensure freedom of worship for his fellow Catholics that civil war threatened. A group of Protestants invited James's Dutch-born nephew and son-in-law, William of Orange, to invade. William agreed and James was compelled to flee the country. A convention in England in February 1689 offered the crown of that kingdom to William and his British-born wife Mary Stuart as joint sovereigns. James meanwhile skulked in France where he was welcomed by Louis XIV. A chateau was placed at his disposal and he was given funds to maintain his court. The French king's motives were simple: to use James's presence to cause trouble for his enemy, William of Orange.

But not everyone back in Britain had disapproved of the exiled king. Those who supported him were known as Jacobites, from Jacobus, Latin for James, and they were to play an important part in British history for the next 60 years. Scotland in particular was divided. The Stuart dynasty had ruled for more than three centuries, and loyalties ran deep, especially in the Highlands. The supporters of James, known as the Jacobites, found a leader in John Graham of Claverhouse, Viscount Dundee (the 'Bonnie Dundee' since commemorated in song). Opposing him was General Hugh MacKay, a veteran soldier who was given command of the government troops in Scotland.

The first shots in the Jacobite cause — a conflict that was to tear Scotland asunder — were about to be fired.

In Edinburgh the parliamentary Convention was engaged in proceedings which were to lead to the Scottish crown being offered to William and Mary. At the same time, Edinburgh Castle was being held for James by the Duke of Gordon. At his home in the city from which he took his title, Viscount Dundee was summoned

*The Pass of Killiecrankie: the 'Queen's view' (**Below**); the 'Soldier's leap' (**Right**).*

to the Convention. He refused to attend and rode out of the city with 50 followers — an action which Sir Walter Scott later immortalised in his poem *Bonny Dundee*.

Dundee set about raising the Highlanders and MacKay, with well-trained cavalry and 3,000 foot soldiers, set out on weeks of fruitless pursuit. Attention focused on Blair Castle, home of the Marquis of Atholl, which was being held by the Jacobites. The castle was strategically important. Whoever held it could command the pass through the hills and the route to the north. So when the news reached Dundee, in Lochaber, and MacKay, in Perth, both marched towards Blair.

Two armies were now on the road that led up Strath Tay to picturesque Pitlochry and onwards to the Pass of Killiecrankie.

On the morning of 27 July 1689, as MacKay's army was making its way through the narrow defile of the pass, Dundee had already reached Blair Castle. Dundee led his troops away from the castle, over the hills behind Blair, and took up position on a south-facing ridge. With only 2,500 men and few horse he needed the advantage of ground. In silver and buff coat, with green scarf, he positioned himself with his small troop of cavalry in the centre of the line. Below, MacKay emerging at the north end of the pass, halted his force on level ground above the River Garry.

For two hours the armies waited. Then, at about seven o'clock on the summer evening, when the sun was no longer in the eyes of his troops, Dundee gave the order to charge. Kilt and plaid in those days were one garment. As was their custom, the men discarded this cumbersome cloak. Clad in their shirts, crouching behind their shields to present the smallest target, they rushed at the enemy.

MacKay's troops were armed with a new weapon, the bayonet. This did not clip on to the muzzle, as it did later, but had to be screwed on. A soldier, having fired his weapon, was expected to perform this awkward operation while his enemy was rapidly approaching wielding a double-edged broadsword. The result was that when the two armies met, all was over in a couple of minutes.

General MacKay wrote of his troops: 'With the exception of Hastings' and Leven's regiments, they behaved like the vilest cowards in nature. In the twinkling of an eye, our men, as well as the enemy, were out of sight, being got down pell-mell to the river.'

With a few scattered remnants, MacKay made his escape. He had lost nearly half his army, 2,000 killed or taken prisoner. The Highland losses were 900 — including, though his men did not at first realise it, Dundee himself. He had been hit in the opening minutes as he turned to urge on the cavalry. Wrapped in two plaids, his body was carried to Blair Castle: he was buried in the old church.

The Highland victory was complete. But for the Jacobites, the battle was an isolated success. The clans regrouped and marched on Dunkeld. But the little town had been occupied by the newly formed Cameronians and, without Dundee to lead them, the victors of Killiecrankie were very soon defeated in a bloody battle on 21 August. The Highlanders' rising against the crown was over — for the time being.

When King James died in 1701, French King Louis sent heralds to the chateau where he had spent his exile to proclaim his 13-year old son King James VIII of Scotland and III of England. The boy was to grow up to become known to history as the 'Old Pretender' (Pretender meaning claimant). And his son, Prince Charles Edward Stuart, was to become known as the 'Young Pretender' — or more popularly 'Bonnie Prince Charlie'.

In 1702 William of Orange also died. His horse stumbled over a molehill and threw him. Jacobites toasted 'the little gentleman in black velvet'. They also had their own version of the loyal toast, passing their wine glasses over water — a silent token that it was to the king over the sea that they drank. It was never easy to estimate the strength of Jacobite support. William of Orange had been unpopular, and exile inevitably increased the attractions of the Stuart monarchy. There were Jacobites in all parts of Britain and they plotted continuously. But not all those who drank to 'the king over the water' were prepared to fight to restore him.

When it did come to real military effort, it was the Highlands of Scotland which consistently provided the largest part of the Jacobite armies. Although not all Highlanders were Jacobites, there were factors which led them to favour the exiled dynasty more than most. One was simple loyalty to a king of Scottish descent. Another was that, since the clans were run on patriarchal lines with chiefs whose word was law, they found nothing untoward in the idea of a despotic king. And, of course, those who were Catholic or Episcopalian had not been repelled, as Protestant clans had been, by James's attacks on their religion.

In 1708 James II's son, now aged 20, made his first bid for the crown. With 6,000 French troops in 30 vessels, he set out from Dunkirk. The fleet anchored in the Firth of Forth. It was the young man's intention to present himself to the Scots as James III, and ask them to break the Treaty of Union with England, which had been arrived at only the previous year. But a superior naval force under Admiral Byng appeared, and the French fled north, to return in disorder to Dunkirk by way of the north of Scotland and Ireland.

Seven years later, James tried again. At his instigation, and in his absence, the Earl of Mar raised the Stuart standard at Braemar on 6 September 1715, proclaiming James, King of Scotland, England, Ireland and France. With nearly 10,000 men, Mar marched south and met George I's army, under the Duke of Argyll, at Sherrifmuir, near Stirling. The battle was indecisive. Mar withdrew to Perth and all initiative was lost. James arrived in Peterhead in December but by this time his support had melted away and Argyll was at his heels. He sailed for France on 4 February 1716, accompanied by the unhappy Mar, and never saw Scotland again.

In England a simultaneous Jacobite rising had also been defeated. On both sides of the border punishment was severe. There were executions — many by the gruesome ritual of hanging, drawing and quartering — sentences of transportation, and the abolition of titles, including 19 Scottish peerages.

Nevertheless, it was only four years later that the next attempt was made. This time it suited Spain, at war with both Britain and France, to play the Jacobite card. A force of 29 ships with 5,000 soldiers and arms for another 30,000 sailed from Cadiz — and was promptly shattered by a storm. An earlier diversionary force, however, including 307 Spaniards, had already sailed. This reached Scotland and made its headquarters in Eilean Donan Castle on Lochalsh. The castle was bombarded by the Royal Navy and its Spanish garrison surrendered. There was little support from the clans, and on 10 June 1719, in the beautiful setting of Glen Shiel, the Jacobite force was defeated by troops from Inverness garrison.

It was to be another 25 years before the next, and last, attempt to put a Stuart on the throne. Meantime the Highlands were changing. Forts were erected and manned. General George Wade, commander-in-chief in Scotland, built some 260 miles of road and 40 bridges to enable government troops to penetrate the mountains. Companies of Highlanders were recruited to maintain order, and were distinguished by their own dark tartan — the origin of the Black Watch. It was against this historically changing background that the drama of the great 'Forty Five' rebellion was to be played.

Right: *The snowy slopes of Kintail.*

BONNIE PRINCE CHARLIE

At Glenfinnan, on the famous 'Road to the Isles', Highland beauty and Highland history again come together. Great mountains guard the narrow length of Loch Shiel. Their wooded slopes rise steeply from its edge. The scene changes with every change of light. At the head of the loch, a narrow strip of land makes a natural stage in the amphitheatre of the hills. Here stands the monument, a 20m (65ft) pillar surmounted by the statue of a Highlander and surrounded by a stone stockade.

It was built in 1815 by Alexander MacDonald of Glenaladale 'to commemorate the generous zeal, the undaunted bravery and the inviolable fidelity of his forefathers and the rest of those who fought and bled in that arduous and unfortunate enterprise'.

It commemorates the day — 19 August 1745 — when on this spot Prince Charles Edward Stuart, 'Bonnie Prince Charlie', raised his standard and heard his father proclaimed King James VIII of Scotland and III of England and Ireland. It was the first act of the dramatic adventure known in history as the 'Forty Five', the last endeavour to regain for the Stuart dynasty the throne of Britain.

It was a romantic spectacle . . . the young Prince, tall, slim and handsome, surrounded by his army of fierce-looking Highlanders. But it was also an act of war against the ruling British monarch in London. It set in motion a train of events which led, eight months later, to the last battle fought on British soil. To Culloden.

It is tempting to view the Forty-Five as a struggle between Scots and English or between Highlanders and non-Highlanders. The reality was different. Religious and political beliefs dictated diverse loyalties, often within clans and even within families. So, as in all civil wars, there was for many combatants that special agony when facing the enemy, of seeing a brother or a son on the other side.

Prince Charles Edward Stuart's army was predominantly Highland, but by no means exclusively so. Not all the clans rallied to his standard. Had they done so, he might well have marched on London at the head of 30,000 men and the course of history would have been changed. The prince's support came mainly from the Roman Catholic and Episcopalian clans. The Campbells, staunchly Presbyterian, fought for the English — but not all, for those from Glen Lyon served in the prince's Atholl Brigade. Cumberland's forces included three Scottish Lowland regiments. There were clansmen who fought only because their homes and families would have suffered had they not answered their chief's call. There were others, Grants and Macleods among them, who rallied to the cause despite their chief's disapproval.

Perhaps the deciding factor in the Forty-Five, however, was the great majority who did not rise — the Highlanders and Lowlanders, Scots and English, who stayed at home and awaited the outcome.

Had all gone as planned, however, the Forty-Five would have been the Forty-Four, and a much more serious threat to George II. In February of that year, Louis XV planned a massive invasion of Britain. His objective was to place on the throne in London a monarch who would be ultimately dependent upon France. Ten thousand regular French troops were assembled at Dunkirk ready to sail to Essex and march on London. But again weather intervened; a storm wrecked the invasion fleet and the expedition was abandoned. The young Prince Charles Edward Stuart, who was to have sailed with the fleet as the Prince of Wales and representative of his father, found that once his potential usefulness to Louis was gone he was virtually ignored.

Prince Charles Edward Stuart — Bonnie Prince Charlie — arrived on mainland Scotland at Loch nan Uamh near Arisaig on 25 July 1745. He raised his standard at Glenfinnan on Loch Shiel on 19 August and set off to reconquer his kingdom. Unlike all good fairy stories, this tale did not have a happy ending and the Forty Five — as the rebellion became known — was to lead the Prince to a life in drunken exile and his Highlanders to death.

Above and Right: *Re-enactment of the arrival of Bonnie Prince Charlie at Glenfinnan and the raising of his standard. His father was declared king, and the rebellion had begun.*

The prince was not so easily put off. On 16 July 1745 he set out on his own expedition with only two ships, seven supporters and a small store of arms and ammunition. Off the west coast of Ireland, the expedition encountered a British man-o'-war which saw off one of the ships (containing the bulk of military stores) while the prince's ship slipped away to the Hebridean island of Eriskay.

The Prince's first contact on Scottish soil was not encouraging. On Eriskay, Alexander MacDonald of Boisdale advised him to go home. 'I am come home, sir,' replied the prince.

On 25 July the prince's ship reached the Scottish mainland at Loch nam Uamh, near Arisaig, from where he sent out letters to Highland chiefs seeking support. At Glenfinnan on 19 August, the standard was raised, his father proclaimed James VIII and III, and the prince himself as regent. The Forty-Five had begun.

It was a small force at first, only about 1,200 men. More than half of them were Camerons, under the chief's son, known to history as 'Gentle Lochiel', the chief, his father being in exile. Most of the remainder were MacDonalds of Keppoch. They gathered strength as they moved eastwards, avoiding the government garrisons at Fort William and Fort Augustus, and crossing by the Corrieyairack Pass into Badenoch, ironically by one of the roads built by General Wade to discourage Highland insurgency. A government army under Lt-Gen Sir John Cope was hurried north but chose not to meet Charles, instead marching to Inverness, so leaving the route south to Edinburgh open to the Jacobites. At Perth, the Prince was joined by Lord George Murray (brother of the Duke of Atholl) who was to prove his outstanding field commander.

Edinburgh was entered virtually unopposed on 17 September, though the castle remained in government hands. The prince occupied the Palace of Holyroodhouse, home of his ancestors. Cope, meanwhile, had marched to Aberdeen and taken ship to Dunbar. He moved towards Edinburgh but on 21 September, in less than 10 minutes, his army was routed at the Battle of Prestonpans.

Charles, magnanimous and humane in victory, was master of Scotland. But it was not enough. On 1 November, in one of the most ambitious military campaigns of history, Prince Charles Edward Stuart turned his army south and began a march on the English capital, London.

Carlisle surrendered on 16 November, 12 days later the army reached Manchester, and on the evening of 4 December, Derby. London was now only 127 miles away and the city was in a state of panic. Catholic support, which had thus far been disappointing, was at last growing throughout England and Wales. Ten thousand French troops were said to be embarking at Dunkirk. A rapier-like thrust at the capital was in prospect.

Such a move could conceivably have succeeded. Charles was all for continuing his march south. But all was not well. The Prince's army had lacked English support, and about a thousand of his Highlanders had quietly left to return to their native glens. Three government armies were threatening to converge on the the Jacobite force. And Charles and Lord George Murray had quarrelled. Cause of the upset was the influence wielded by one of the prince's original seven supporters who had been a thorn in Lord George's side during the entire campaign, and was responsible for much of its failure. He was Irishman John William O'Sullivan, the army's adjutant and quartermaster-general, a great favourite of the prince, and — in Lord George's opinion — an idiot.

On 6 December — 'Black Friday' — the prince took the decision to retreat. It may have been a wrong one. Dispirited, his troops faced the long road back to Scotland.

Glasgow was reached on Christmas Day, but the city was ill-disposed. Only Lochiel's intervention saved it from being sacked, a circumstance which in later years, tradition says, led to the bells being rung whenever the chief of Clan Cameron entered the city.

Stirling town surrendered but not the castle. Reinforcements arrived, including 400 from Clan Mackintosh raised by Lady Macintosh (the redoubtable 'Colonel Anne') whose husband, head of the clan, was on the government side. Men, stores and ammunition arrived from France. From Edinburgh, Lt-Gen Hawley marched to relieve Stirling. The battle of Falkirk, on 17 January, was a victory for the prince's army, but in the confusion of a winter dusk the advantage was neither realised nor exploited. Hawley retired to Edinburgh, there to hang his deserters on gallows erected for Jacobites, while the Prince's army trudged north to Inverness.

Above and Right: *Loch Shiel and the Glenfinnan Monument to the Forty Five. Built in 1815, it stands at the head of the loch, but a few miles from Fort William — one of the obvious signs of Hanoverian oppression of the Highlands. Fort William was not to fall to the rebels, but all the other strongholds were — severely denting the pride of the English who had thought them sufficient after the 1715 rebellion. In fact much vaunted Fort Augustus fell after a two-day siege and the Highlanders made much better use than the English of Wade's roads which were supposed to assist King George's army.*

At Prestonpans, just outside Edinburgh, Prince Charles won an initial victory which gave heart and credibility to the revolt. But for all the derogaotry comments made about George II (1727-60) he was no pushover: he was the last British monarch to lead his troops into battle (at Dettingen in 1743) and would not give up the Scottish crown lightly.

There were sporadic actions. The Jacobites took Fort Augustus, at the foot of Loch Ness, and near Dornoch defeated government troops under Lord Loudon, who had retreated from Inverness. One of the prisoners taken was the Mackintosh chief, whom Prince Charles gallantly returned to his home, Moy Hall — and to 'Colonel Anne', his wife. It is said that when the chief arrived home, his wife greeted him with: 'At your service Captain.' To which he replied: 'No, at your service, Colonel.'

There was a major setback for the Jacobites, however, when a captured government sloop, dispatched to France to seek support was taken by the English navy off the Kyle of Tongue. Her vital hoard of much needed gold and stores never reached the prince.

Meanwhile, the Duke of Cumberland, second son of George II and, despite his youth, an experienced commander, had built up a formidable army at Aberdeen, reinforced by 5,000 Germans under Prince Frederick of Hesse. Cumberland left Aberdeen on 8 April and six days later, to the surprise of the Jacobites sheltering in Inverness, he had arrived in the neighbouring town of Nairn.

On 14 April the drums beat and the pipes sounded to assemble the Jacobite army for battle. Messengers were sent out to recall the many who were on forays elsewhere. Next day, on the moor which was then called Drumossie but is now Culloden, the army was drawn up in the order in which it was to fight the coming battle.

Above and Right: *Until the accession of Edward VII to the British throne in 1901, fingerbowls were never placed on royal dinner tables so as not to allow the secret Jacobite supporters to drink to the 'king over the water'. There were other symbols of support for the Stuart dynasty but when push came to shove most of the Lowlanders and English supporters of the rising sat on the fence to see who was going to win rather than get burnt.*

Apart from the obvious suitability of location it is therefore apposite that the monument to the rebellion allows Prince Charles to gaze over the Highlands whose sons were ever his support in battle and who felt the backlash of the English establishment in the years to come.

CULLODEN

No place name in Scottish history stirs the emotions more than Culloden. Fought on 16 April 1746, it has all the elements of romantic fiction, all the appeal of a lost cause. It has a hero: young dashing, handsome Prince Charles Edward Stuart, the 'Bonnie Prince Charlie' of song and story. And it has a villain: the brutal Duke of Cumberland, of whom no one now sings.

On the eve of that battle, however, some were indeed singing the praises of Cumberland — but only in drunken revelry. On Tuesday 15 April, the duke was celebrating his 25th birthday, and his men, in camp around Nairn, were drinking his health in brandy.

By a strange irony, these jollifications had some bearing on the battle the following day. As the Prince's army waited at Culloden, his commander Lord George Murray proposed a night attack on the English camp. The celebrating soldiers would be 'drunk as beggars,' he said. The Prince agreed and sent out two columns to catch Cumberland unawares. But their progress across the wastes of Culloden — then known as Drumossie Moor — took so long that dawn was breaking before they could mount their attack. They discovered that Cumberland had broken camp at 5am and, the nocturnal expedition aborted, the clansmen returned to the royal lines with the English army hot on their heels.

Cold, hungry and dispirited, the apprehensive Scots now peered out across the boggy, featureless field of battle to face the hung-over but buoyant English. Lord George Murray was to write later: 'There could never be a more improper ground for Highlanders'. It was not he who had chosen it but the Prince's favourite, John William O'Sullivan, against the urgings of Lord George.

The prince ordered his men to be drawn up, as on the previous day, those on foot in two lines, his weak cavalry in the rear, and his meagre artillery — 13 assorted guns — in three batteries on the right, left and in the centre of the front line. His force was small, under 5,000 men. Detachments on tasks elsewhere had been recalled but not all arrived in time. Among them were the MacPhersons who had only reached Moy Hall at the time of the battle. Many men had gone off in search of food; others, exhausted, were asleep.

Cumberland had nearly 9,000 men — 6,500 foot, including 15 regular regiments, and 2,400 horse, including 800 mounted dragoons. His artillery consisted of 10 three-pounder guns and six mortars. The army force-marched from Nairn to Culloden in three columns, with the cavalry on its left and a screen of Campbell scouts in front.

At 11am the two armies came in sight of each other. Cumberland's three columns wheeled around as if they were on a parade ground, not a boggy moor, and within 10 minutes were facing the Jacobites.

Charles looked every inch the prince as he rode on his fine, grey gelding, in his tartan coat and cockaded bonnet, carrying a light broadsword, and encouraging his men. His front line consisted almost entirely of clansmen, standing from three to six deep.The Jacobite second line was perhaps 100 yards behind, and was much shorter. The contrast between the smart, well-fed English army and the plaid-clad, ill-provisioned Scots must have been stark.

The Highlanders were outnumbered, 5,000 against Cumberland's 9,000, and were destined to die in disproportionate numbers, more than 1,000 against Cumberland's 364. They were ill equipped, their artillery poor, their cavalry few. They were exhausted, having marched all night on an abortive foray. They were hungry, because poor staff work had left their food supplies in Inverness. They were badly led, being required to fight over ground which suited Cumberland's cannon and cavalry and handicapped their main tactic — the charge. Yet they went into battle with a courage which has passed into legend, and which today Scots the world over still salute.

Above and Right: *Re-enactment of the battle of Culloden.*

Opposing Bonnie Prince Charlie was, perhaps had he known it, a reason for hope — his adversary William Augustus Duke of Cumberland (1721-65). The second surviving son of George Augustus, Prince of Wales who would become George II in 1727 on the death of his father, Cumberland was made major-general in 1742 at the age of 21. A brave man — he fought with distinction at Dettingen in 1743 — he was promoted captain-general of all British land forces in 1745 and was fighting on the continent when the rebellion began.

Unfortunately while he may have been brave, he was also unimaginative, unlucky and some would say incompetent as a general. Apart from victory over the Highlanders at Culloden, he lost with regularity to the French at Fontenoy in 1745, Lauffeld in 1747 and Hastenbeck in 1757 and finally retired in disgrace.

The first shots fired came from a Jacobite gun, and it is said one of them narrowly missed the duke. There was to be no artillery duel however. The English guns returned fire with devastating effect. The round shot cut swathes in the Highland ranks. The Jacobite guns answered ineffectually. With wind, sleet and the enemy gunsmoke blowing in their faces, the long tartan-clad line could do nothing but stand and suffer the slaughter. The ranks were often six deep, and a cannonball could mangle several men. This was not the kind of warfare to which the Highlanders were accustomed.

Some fire was directed over their heads at the prince and his command group; his servant was killed, and his horse shot from under him. The prince was too far in the rear to see what was happening and, despite the murderous barrage, still the order to charge — the word 'Claymore' — was not given. And when the charge did come, it was not what it should have been: a wild, terrifying rush by the whole Highland line.

Yelling their war cries, the clansmen came on; broadswords, axes, scythe blades waving. The carnage was appalling. Only on the right did the charge go home, and there the clansmen had to climb over their dead and wounded to get at the enemy. Elsewhere, the rush did not reach the enemy ranks. Grape-shot and musketry halted the tide. Lord George Murray fought his way to the rear of the duke's army, his wig and his hat blown from his head. He saw what was happening, fought his way back, intending to bring up the Highland second line. But by this time it was over. Defiant, but defeated, the clansmen were moving back. The moor over which they had fought was covered with dead and wounded. The rout was complete.

The prince, bewildered and distressed, some say in tears, was led on horseback from the field. The conflict had lasted less than an hour. But more than a battle had been lost that day. The Jacobite cause was irretrievably in ruins. And its aftermath was to effect the whole future of the Highlands.

What little remained intact of the prince's army withdrew in good order under Lord George Murray, towards Ruthven, in Badenoch. There, the next day, cold comfort awaited them: a message from Charles that each man should save himself.

Worse remained for those who had not managed to flee Culloden. For on the battlefield and beyond, there was being enacted a systematic process of murder and mutilation which an English historian was to describe as 'such as never perhaps before or since disgraced a British army'. On the moor with its dead and wounded, and on the road to Inverness packed with fugitives, Cumberland's dragoons slaughtered indiscriminately — and not only the fleeing clansmen. Innocent bystanders, including women and children, were sabred, and there were casual murders, as of a man who was ploughing and his nine-year old son.

On the battlefield, surgeons cared for the government wounded — while redcoats, watched by their officers, bayonetted or clubbed to death the wounded of the prince's army, often obscenely mutilating their bodies.

There were still men who resisted and whose bravery has passed into Highland legend. Gillies MacBean of Clan Chattan, badly wounded but with his back to a wall and broadsword in his hand, is said to have killed 13 of the enemy before the horses of the dragoons trampled him underfoot. Even then he did not die, but crawled to a barn at Balvraid where he lived until evening.

The Cameron standard-bearer, MacLachlan of Coruanan,

wrapped the flag of his clan round his body as he withdrew. This is believed to be the old stained flag which still hangs in Achnacarry, seat of Lochiel, Chief of the Clan. The courage of the men of Clan Cameron, who carried their wounded chief from the field, was matched by that of Iain Garbh Cameron who bore the wounded Grant of Corriemony on his back all the way to Glenurquart, on faraway Loch Ness.

The stories of heroism and of brutality are legion. One of the best known is told of Cumberland himself. He asked a badly wounded man to which side he belonged, and being told 'to the prince', turned to one of his aides, a Major Wolfe, and ordered him to kill 'the insolent rebel'. Wolfe refused, saying he would rather resign his commission. A private soldier was found who obeyed the order. The murdered man was Charles Fraser, of Inverallochy, commander of the Fraser contingent, and it is said that General Wolfe's popularity in Canada among the Highlanders of his army, and in particular the Fraser regiment, stemmed from this incident.

Through acts such as these, Cumberland won the nickname the 'Butcher' — and it did not entirely come from his victims. One of his own officers wrote in a letter that the men engaged in the slaughter on the Moor 'looked like so many butchers rather than Christian soldiers'.

Cumberland issued an order to seek out surviving rebels, stating ominously: 'The officers and men will take notice that the public orders of the rebels yesterday was to give no quarter.' It was a lie. Lord George Murray's orders for the battle contained no such instruction — a copy of those orders having been captured and the 'no quarter' phrase added as a clumsy forgery.

But it served its purpose. The killing continued for days as the search parties discovered survivors, mostly wounded, in their hiding places. They found more than 30 officers and men in a barn on Old Leanach farm, barricaded it and set it alight. A woman who had given shelter to another 12 watched as they were led away by redcoats who had promised them medical attention. They were shot within yards of her house. A widow returning from burying her husband in Inverness found 16 dead men at her door . . .

Cumberland returned to London in triumph. The self-styled 'deliverer of this Church and Nation' had the flower 'Sweet William' named after him (the Scots retaliated by christening a weed 'Stinking William'). From the rarefied atmosphere of the English court, he advocated his own 'final solution' to the Highland problem: the transportation of whole clans 'such as the Camerons and almost all the tribes of the MacDonalds (excepting some of those in the Isles) and several other lesser clans'.

On his orders, the process of laying waste the glens began. Garrisons at Inverness, nearby Fort George, at Fort Augustus and at Fort William looted, demolished houses, stole horses, cattle and sheep. The Highlands had never been rich; now many of its people faced starvation.

Prince Charles Edward Stuart was little better off himself. There was a £30,000 price on the head of this fugitive in the heather but it failed to bring forth a single informant. The search for him was unremitting; thousands of troops and a small fleet were engaged.

Accompanied by only two or three companions, he hid in Scotland's north-west Highlands and Islands. Flora Macdonald, whose father was with the government forces, gained everlasting fame by conveying him 'over the sea to Skye'. From 'safe houses' in South Uist and the Isle of Skye, he eventually returned to the mainland, hungry, bitten by lice and midges and suffering from dysentery. Yet from those who shared his hardships he won golden opinions for his courage and gaiety. Finally, at Loch nan Uamh, where he had landed 14 months earlier, he boarded *L'Heureux* and sailed for France.

Above and Above Right: *Re-enactment of the battle.*

Below Right: *Culloden Moor. The last pitched battle on British soil would see 1,000 Highlanders lost for about 50 English casualties. In conditions that did not suit their fighting strengths, harried by accurate and sustained artillery fire, tired after a long night march, the Highlanders succumbed on that bloody April day in 1746 and the hopes of their prince died with them.*

'Bonnie Prince Charlie' was to live for another 42 years and die, drunken and dissolute, in Rome. But in the few brief months when he flashed across the pages of history, he created an enduring legend. Jacobitism was to become a romantic, nostalgic cause, enshrined in a wealth of song and story, as it continues to be today.

The actual story of the Highlanders is less lyrical. In London, the Privy Council decided that prisoners be tried in England, a flagrant breach of the Treaty of Union between Scotland and England. The result was that 120 prisoners were executed; four of them, peers of the realm, being beheaded, as was the privilege of their rank, and the rest suffering the barbaric ritual of hanging, drawing and quartering. Another 936 were transported to the colonies, there to be sold to the highest bidder; 222 were banished, being allowed to chose their country of exile: 1,287 were released, exchanged or pardoned, and there were nearly 700 whose fate is unknown.

But this was far from the end. The spectacle of the Highlander, armed and again in rebellion, haunted the government. It had to be eradicated and it was. The so-called Disarming Acts demanded that all weapons be surrendered. Bagpipes too, were a weapon of war, a court in York decreed, and had the piper executed. Wearing tartan, a kilt 'or any part whatever of what peculiarly belongs to the Highland garb' was outlawed, the penalty being six months' imprisonment or, for a second offence, transportation for seven years. Most damaging to the Highland way of life, however, was the Heritable Jurisdictions Act of 1747 removing from clan chiefs their

hereditary powers and turning them into mere landlords. Their wealth had been reckoned in men, and now, with the dissolution of the clan system, men were no longer important.

Twenty-seven years after the Battle of Culloden, the English diarist Dr Samuel Johnson, himself no lover of the Scots, travelled through much of the country and, in his *Journey to the Western Isles*, wrote: 'It affords a legislator little self applause that where there was formerly an insurrection there is now a wilderness.'

The Highland way of life had for ever been eradicated.

Right: *Aerial view of the battlefield of Culloden.*

Far Right: *One of the immediate consequences of Culloden was the hounding of the clans and the determination of the English that there should be no repetition of the lack of success enjoyed by the small forts erected after the Old Pretender's rebellion of 1715. Fort George was to be a base for the exercise of Hanoverian might. It's a wonderful study of the art of military fortification of the time — but it was destined to be a waste of money. So cowed were the Highlanders, that by the time work finished on it in 1769 it was virtually redundant: by 1795 it was garrisoned by a company of soldiers unfit for active service.*

Below: *Old Leanach cottage, Culloden.*

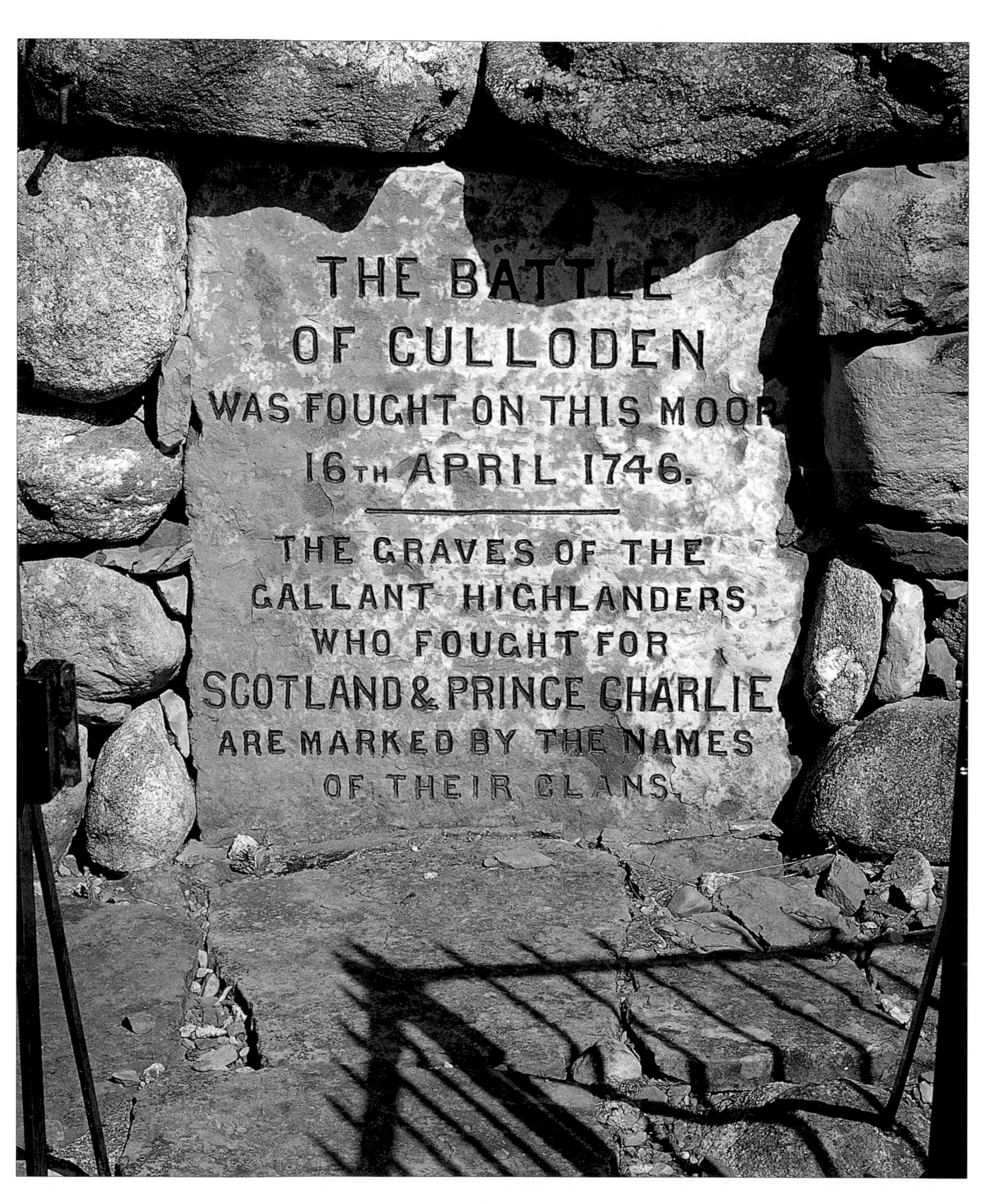

Above and Right: *The Culloden Memorial Cairn. It reads: 'The Battle of Culloden was fought here on 16 April 1746. The graves of the gallant highlanders who fought for Scotland & Prince Charlie are marked by the names of their clans.'*

THE BATTLE
OF CULLODEN
WAS FOUGHT ON THIS MOOR
16TH APRIL 1746.
THE GRAVES OF THE
GALLANT HIGHLANDERS
WHO FOUGHT FOR
SCOTLAND & PRINCE CHARLIE
ARE MARKED BY THE NAMES
OF THEIR CLANS.

Above: *Fort George detail.*

Right: *Fort George is built on a promontory into the Moray Firth near Nairn and opposite Fortrose. Its great bastions epitomised 18th century military architecture and even the great General Wolfe, when still a colonel, was moved to call it 'the most considerable fortress and the best situated in Great Britain'.*

Gun emplacement at Fort George, looking out at the Moray Firth.

Above and Right: *Bonnie Prince Charlie's immortality was assured before he fled the field at Culloden: but the romance was increased many more times by the story of his escape. Despite a price of £30,000 on his head and an unremitting search, he was hidden in farm houses and made a circuitous route through the Highlands and Western Isles before eventual safety . . . and a death in 1788 in exile.*

However the Stuart line did not die out immediately: his claim to the throne passed, on his death, to his brother Henry (who would have been Henry IX) a Catholic cardinal who died in1807. The claim then reverted to the descendants of Charles II's sister Henrietta, Duchess of Orleans and in 1914 the Jacobite monarch of Britain would have been the eminently unsuitable Queen of Bavaria.

Left: *The Clan Cameron memorial on Culloden Moor.*

Below: *The Clan Mackintosh memorial on Culloden Moor.*

JEWEL OF SCOTLAND

In this story of Ancient Scotland, we have skirted around the abiding jewel in her crown: Edinburgh, the capital, the centre of government, the living heart of the nation's history.

The past is still a vibrant, living reality in the city of Edinburgh. Here is the focus for discovering how people throughout the centuries lived and worked in a city and its surrounding countryside. Edinburgh is famous the world over for its magnificent architecture and there is every style from every age. Here stand royal apartments and stately homes filled with antiques, artifacts and tales of intrigue and glory. The footsteps of the celebrated and infamous can be followed along Europe's most historic street, the Royal Mile. And at the end of the Royal Mile lie the Scottish crown jewels — the so-called 'Honours of Scotland' — which have been kept safe for centuries within the protective walls of Edinburgh Castle. This massive edifice, through its every stone, tells the history of the nation of which it is an emblem.

Edinburgh Castle stands boldly atop a dramatic outcrop of volcanic rock born more than 340 million years ago following a violent eruption deep in the earth's crust. Man may first have stood on the Castle Rock about 8,000 years ago when Stone Age hunters and gatherers appeared in the densely-wooded and boggy landscape.

However, its story as a place of permanent human habitation stretches back a 'mere' 3,000 years, to the late Bronze Age. Recent excavations have uncovered evidence for a settlement of round houses on the rock dating to the late Bronze Age (about 900 BC).

It was evidently a thriving hilltop settlement when Roman soldiers marched by in the 1st century AD and returned during the second, by which date the empire had established its most northerly frontier, the Antonine Wall (built in AD 142-3), to the west of Edinburgh. Archaeologists have found a wealth of Roman material, suggesting close contact between the Roman military and the native Votadini tribe.

Above: *Sunset over Edinburgh Castle — palace, treasury, refuge and prison for Scottish monarchs from the 11th century when Malcolm III built the first wooden fortress.*

Below: *The castle's dominating position on its 80m (270ft) rock above Edinburgh gave it enormous strategic importance throughout the years..*

Above Right: *In the distance, the castle can be seen across Princes Street gardens and the railway line. At right the fume-blackened Scott memorial and Princes Street.*

Below Right: *A similar view at dusk looking over busy Princes Street towards the castle. The Scottish Baronial clock tower of the North British hotel flies the Cross of St Andrew.*

But the first recorded mention of a town on the present-day site is not until shortly before AD 600, by which time the Votadini tribe had come to be known as the Gododdin. The war band of the Gododdin was gathered with its king, Mynyddog Mwynfawr, on Castle Rock — or Din Eidyn, 'the stronghold of Eidyn', as it was then known. In the taper-lit hall the 300 men with the bard Andiron pledged themselves in drink to die in the service of their lord. And all but a few did die, on a raid into the territories of the Angles in about AD 600, at Catraeth (Catterick in Yorkshire). Retreating to their tribal lands, the Gododdin were pursued by the Angles. Din Eidyn was besieged and taken in 638, and the place seems then to have received the English name, Edinburgh, which it has kept ever since.

By 1000 AD Edinburgh had become an important fortress. In 1018 King Malcolm II defeated the English at the Battle of Carham

and firmly secured for Scotland the territory between the Firth of Forth and the River Tweed. A royal castle at Edinburgh first emerges at the end of that century.

In 1093 Queen Margaret, seriously ill in Edinburgh Castle, returned to her chamber from Mass to be told of the killing of her husband, King Malcolm III, by the English at the Battle of Alnwick. The news caused her death and her body was taken out of the castle through the western postern gate and buried in Dunfermline Abbey, Fife.

By the reign of Malcolm and Margaret's youngest son, King David I (1124-53), the rocky summit was a thriving royal castle, serving as a court residence, as a storehouse, as the headquarters of the town's sheriff and as a prison. David was probably responsible for the earliest surviving building on the Castle Rock: the little Romanesque chapel later dedicated to his mother, who was canonised as St Margaret in 1250.

With the exception of St Margaret's Chapel, nothing survives of the early royal castle. The reason, as ever, was the conflict between Scotland and her power-hungry southern neighbour.

In 1296 King Edward I of England invaded and Edinburgh Castle soon fell into his hands. But after his death in 1307 the English grasp on Scotland weakened, and in 1314 a night attack led by Robert the Bruce's forces recaptured the castle. It was a daring plan which involved 30 hand-picked men making the seemingly impossible ascent of the north precipice and taking the garrison by surprise. Bruce immediately ordered the dismantling of the defences to prevent reoccupation by the English. Shortly after, Bruce's army routed the English at Bannockburn.

After Bruce's death and his succession by his son David II in 1329, hostilities again broke out and in 1335 the castle once more fell into English hands. Major repairs were carried out but these proved ineffective against another storybook assault by the Scots, in 1341. A raiding party, disguised as merchants bringing supplies to the garrison, managed to drop its loads at the castle gates, so preventing their closure. A larger force hidden nearby rushed to join them and the castle was taken. Most of the English garrison had their throats cut or their heads chopped off and their bodies thrown over the crags.

In 1356 King David returned to Scotland from a 10-year captivity in England and straightaway set about rebuilding his castle at Edinburgh. A massive, L-shaped tower house rose about 30m (100ft) above the eastern crags. Subsequently named David's Tower, it was intended as a secure royal lodging as well as the main defence towards the burgh. It was battered by cannon during the so-called Lang Siege of 1571-3 and it survives only as a ruin, entombed within the Half-Moon Battery which replaced it as the chief defence on the eastern side of the castle.

King David died in 1371 without seeing his great tower completed. It was left to his successor King Robert II, the first Stewart monarch, to continue the rebuilding work. In 1433 work began on a new Great Chamber for King James I. This building, intended to complement the restricted accommodation within David's Tower, may still remain, albeit greatly altered, in the two 17th century rooms in the present palace now called the 'King's Dining Room' and its anteroom. It was either in the Great Chamber or in the hall in David's Tower that one of the most dastardly episodes in the castle's history took place — the 'Black Dinner' of 1440.

King James II had succeeded his murdered father, King James I, in 1437. A youngster, he was in the care of Sir William Crichton, Keeper of Edinburgh Castle, who used his powerful position in a spectacular political assassination of his political rivals, the Douglas family. Crichton invited the Earl of Douglas, a teenager himself, and his younger brother to dine with the king in the castle. The two guests were greeted:

'With great joy and gladness. [They] banqueted royally with all delicacies that could be got [and] after great cheer was made at the dinner and the courses taken away [Crichton] presented a bull's head before the earl which was a sign and token of condemnation to death.'

The young king protested at this outrage but to no effect. The Douglas's were taken to an adjacent chamber, summarily tried on a trumped-up charge treason and beheaded in the castle courtyard.

In 1457 King James II, now ruling in person, was given a present of two giant siege guns (called 'bombards') by his uncle-by-marriage, Philip the Good, Duke of Burgundy. One of the guns survives in the castle vaults. This is *Mons Meg*, made at Mons, in present-day Belgium. Weighing over 6,040kg (6 tons), it could fire gunstones weighing 150kg (330lb) a full 3.2km (2 miles).

Throughout the Middle Ages, as we can see, Edinburgh had boasted one of the major castles of the kingdom and its story is very much the story of Scotland. Outside the castle, Edinburgh already existed as a royal burgh, but not the most important or the largest in Scotland. Only in the later half of the 15th century, during the reign of King James III from 1460-88, could it be called the capital city of the country. At that time — and for centuries afterwards — it was a dirty, smelly, often plague-ridden town, chronically short of fresh water and prey to vagabonds and villains both in the streets and tenements and in the offices of local government. Its inhabitants would throw open their windows to the fetid air only to empty their chamberpots into the streets below with a cry of 'Garyloo!' — a corruption of the French *gare l'eau*, or 'mind the water'.

No wonder that, under James III, efforts were made to convert Edinburgh Castle into a relatively clean and safe sanctuary; indeed into a renaissance palace. The castle was replanned with, as its focal point, a new courtyard, now called Crown Square, around which was placed the principal royal accommodation. The creation of Crown Square was a huge task involving the construction of massive stone vaults over the whole of the basalt rock platform sloping southwards from St Mary's Church. The Palace and St Mary's Church already stood along the east and north sides of the new courtyard. Along the west side was placed the Gunhouse, where the royal artillery was displayed. The south side was occupied by the Great Hall, the principal banqueting and reception room. This greatly restored but still impressive building was probably completed late in the reign of King James IV (1488-1513).

By the time of King James's death, on the bloody battlefield of Flodden, Edinburgh Castle was the principal royal castle in the realm. It was a formidable fortress, a royal place, the chief arsenal, a treasury for the crown jewels, the repository of the national archives, the residence of several officers of state including the treasurer, and a state prison.

As a prison it was not entirely escape proof as Alexander, the Duke of Albany and King James III's brother, proved in 1479. After killing his guards, Albany lowered himself down the rock on a rope tied to his window. His companion slipped and injured himself, but Albany carried him to the port of Leith and freedom.

The castle on the rock was never the most comfortable or healthy of royal residences. In the 13th century, King Alexander

Above: *Edinburgh Castle and the old town.*

III's young queen, Margaret, described it as a 'sad and solitary place, without greenery and, because of its nearness to the sea, unwholesome' — a reference to the thick sea mist which still envelopes the castle from time to time. Nevertheless, it was the foremost castle of the land and in 1566 was chosen as the place where Mary Queen of Scots should give birth to her first and only child: Prince James, the infant who in time would unite the crowns of Scotland and England as King James VI of Scotland and I of England.

She did not languish in the castle longer than she could help, however, because a newer and more pleasant royal household was being developed just down the road, at the far end of the Royal Mile. The Palace of Holyrood House, which to this day is the official residence in Scotland of the reigning British monarch, was begun in the early 16th century by enlarging a guesthouse of the nearby abbey. The interiors which have modern visitors marvelling, however, were added later, most in the 1670s by the architect Sir William Bruce but many earlier decorations were commissioned by Charles II. They include the extraordinary Royal Portrait Gallery, with 110 Scottish kings and queens painted in 'large royal postures' by a single artist, George de Witt, between 1684 and 1686.

Leading from the picture gallery are the Audience Chamber and the private apartments of Mary Queen Of Scots — scene of one of the best documented murders in history, when Mary's favourite, Rizzio, was stabbed to death by her husband Darnley's accomplices. And although, for reasons of state, she was persuaded to have her son, James VI of Scotland, born in Edinburgh Castle, it was at Holyrood that he learned that he was also to become James I of England, the monarch of two kingdoms.

When Mary was forced to abdicate, there were still those in Scotland who continued to support her cause. Amongst them was Sir William Kirkcaldy of Grange, Keeper of Edinburgh Castle. By the summer of 1571 he was defiantly holding the fortress against the regent governing on behalf of the infant King James. A rather desultory siege of the castle continued for well over a year (hence its name: the Lang Siege) until in 1573 Regent Morton sought help from Queen Elizabeth I of England. An English agent reported that 'there is no mining that can prevail in this rock but only battery with ordnance to beat down the walls'.

Heavy guns were duly dispatched by sea from Berwick and six batteries were set up outside the castle. Within 10 days of the massive bombardment opening up on 16 May, much of the east side of the castle had been reduced to rubble, including most of David's Tower, the Constable's Tower and the stretch of wall in between. The east elevation of the palace, where King James VI had been born just seven years earlier, was badly damaged and its three fine oriel windows largely destroyed. With the main water supply choked by the collapse of David's Tower, Kirkcaldy of Grange had no option but to surrender. He was hanged for treason afterwards.

In 1603 Queen Elizabeth of England died unmarried and without children. Her heir was King James VI of Scotland, descended from her grandfather. The new monarch headed south for London, returning only once, in 1617. In advance of this royal 'hamecoming', the castle was again refurbished, the showpiece being the east front, facing the Old Town. Unlike the other sides, which were of rubble masonry, this side was finely constructed, with parapets, mullioned windows and ornamental panels, including one displaying the 'Honours of Scotland' — of which more later.

With continuing improvements made to the Palace of Holyroodhouse, at the far end of the Royal Mile, Edinburgh Castle was used less and less as a royal residence. But despite the obvious amenities and domestic advantages of Holyrood, the castle remained symbolically the heart of the kingdom. Efforts continued to be made to secure the defences of 'the first and principal strength of the realm' but scant attention was given to the royal accommodation. The last occasion a reigning monarch slept in the castle was when King Charles I, on his only visit, spent the night there before his coronation as King of Scots in 1663. After that, the castle increasingly became the centre of the military arm of government. Almost all the medieval buildings were either converted to military use or demolished, and the old medieval defences were replaced by new artillery fortifications.

King Charles's execution and the unequivocal Scottish support for his rightful successor, King Charles II, brought Oliver Cromwell to Scotland. By Christmas day 1650, the English Roundheads had set up their headquarters in Edinburgh Castle and Cromwell's creation of a permanent standing army was to transform the ancient Royal Castle into a garrison fortress. When King Charles returned to his throne in 1660 he continued the idea of a regular, paid army, and from then until the 20th century a permanent garrison of soldiers was stationed in the castle.

The last time they were called upon to defend their fortress was during the Jacobite risings. In 1715 the Jacobites actually broke through the castle's western perimeter, following which most of the artillery defences now seen protecting the castle on its north and west sides were built. They were soon put to the test during the 1745 rising, but only in a desultory fashion. Bonnie Prince Charlie held court briefly at Holyrood, at the other end of the Royal Mile. His halfhearted effort to take the fortress proved to be the last military action that the castle ever saw.

Yet the ghosts of Edinburgh Castle's violent past remain. In 1689 the Duke of Gordon unsuccessfully held the castle for the exiled King James VII against the forces of William and Mary. The ordinary soldiers who defended the fortress are nowhere recorded. But recently unearthed beside the Old Guardhouse were some bones — the skeletons of 15 well-built men, believed to have been soldiers serving in the garrison at that time. As is so often the case throughout Scottish history, the poor soldiers who fought so defiantly but in vain for their native Scottish soil are remembered only by their bones.

There is one more, very obvious reminder of the military might that was once wielded from within the forbidding stone walls of Edinburgh Castle. From the battlements high above the heads of the citizens of the capital, at precisely one o'clock every afternoon, a signal gun fires a single shot. Visitors jump in fright. Locals simply check their watches . . . as another day passes into the astonishing, tragic, dramatic, glamourous and glorious history of Scotland.

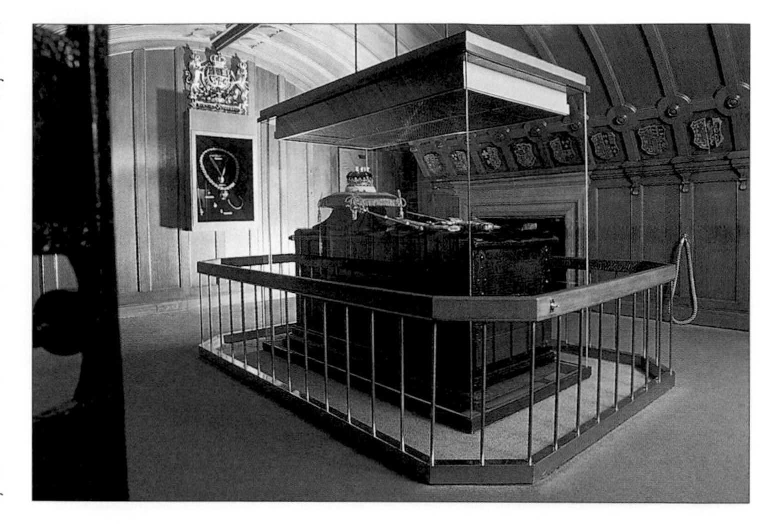

Above: *The Jewels of Scotland in the Old Crown Room of Edinburgh Castle.* *(See page 136.)*

Below Left: *Holyroodhouse got its name when the 11th century queen who was to become St Margaret of Scotland died here leaving her son David a relic of the true cross — a 'holy rood'. Today's palace was started in the early 16th century by James V. After the Restoration Charles II had major works undertaken including the portraits of 89 Scottish monarchs by Dutch artist Jacob de Witt. The oldest rooms are those occupied by Mary Queen of Scots — the James IV tower where her lover Rizzio was murdered.*

Right: *Aerial view of Holyroodhouse Palace showing the park beyond. The highest point in the park is Arthur's Seat at 250m (823ft).*

CASTLE ROCK

The Castle Rock and the Royal Mile are perhaps the world's best example of the geological feature known as the 'crag and tail'. Its origin goes back about 340 million years. Hot molten rock rose through the earth's crust and spread ash and lava over the landscape to form a huge cone-shaped volcano. In time the volcano became extinct

Millions of years later great sheets of ice came and eroded the soft sedimentary rocks that had by this time covered the volcano. The last Ice Age, some 10,000 to 20,000 years ago, was so powerful that it removed almost everything but the volcano's solid basalt feeder pipe. The ice, moving from west to east, flowed around the obstacle and gouged out the area to the west. But the hard basalt protected the softer sediments to its east, and by the time the streams of ice merged once more near the site of Holyrood Palace, the 'crag and tail' — the Castle Rock and Edinburgh's Royal Mile — had been created.

HONOURS OF SCOTLAND

The refurbishment of the palace of Edinburgh Castle for the 'hamecoming' of James VI in 1617 included the provision of a strongroom to house the Scottish crown jewels, known as the 'Honours of Scotland'. The Crown Room still houses these gems, the oldest regalia in the United Kingdom and amongst the oldest surviving in the whole of Christendom.

The Honours of Scotland — the Crown, Sword and Sceptre — were shaped in Italy and Scotland during the reigns of King James IV and King James V and were first used together as coronation regalia at the enthronement of the infant Queen Mary in Stirling Castle in September 1543.

From the time they were taken from Edinburgh Castle in 1650 to be used at the coronation of King Charles II at Scone on New Year's day 1651, they have had an eventful history.

Between 1651 and 1660 they were preserved from capture by Cromwell's army, at first in Dunnottar Castle on the Kincardineshire coast and then, with Dunnottar besieged, smuggled out by the wife of the minister of nearby Kinneff Church, and buried under the church floor.

After the 1707 Treaty of Union between Scotland and England, the Honours were locked away in the Crown Room and the doors walled up. The barricaded room became something of a mystery to the soldiers serving in the garrison.

No less than 111 years later, romantic poet and novelist Sir Walter Scott, with the permission of the Prince Regent (the future King George IV), had the room unblocked and the chest forced open. Scott himself tells the story:

'The chest seemed to return a hollow and empty sound to the strokes of the hammer, and even those whose expectations had been most sanguine felt at the moment the probability of disappointment. The joy was therefore extreme when, he ponderous lid of the chest being forced open, the Regalia were discovered lying at the bottom covered with linen cloths, exactly as they had been left in the year 1707.

'The reliques were passed from hand to hand, and greeted with the affectionate reverence which emblems so venerable, restored to public view after the slumber of more than a hundred years, were so peculiarly calculated to excite.

'The discovery was instantly communicated to the public by the display of the Royal Standard, and was greeted by shouts of the soldiers in the garrison, and a vast multitude assembled on Castle Hill. Indeed the rejoicing was so general and sincere as plainly to show that, however altered in other respects, the people of Scotland had lost nothing of that national enthusiasm which formerly had displayed itself in grief for the loss of these emblematic Honours, and now was expressed in joy for their recovery.'

Except for a period during World War 2, when they were buried once again, this time in David's Tower, the crown, sword and sceptre have remained on display ever since — a proud reminder of Scotland's glittering royal past. Of Scotland's Honour.

NATIONAL TRUST FOR SCOTLAND INDEX
Scenes and sites of Ancient Scotland
administered by the National Trust For Scotland
(5 Charlotte Square, Edinburgh EH2 4DU)

Antonine Wall, three sections of Roman wall and ditches, near Falkirk (under guardianship of Historic Scotland).
Balmerino Abbey, 13th century Cistercian, near Newport-on-Tay.
Bannockburn, an important historic sites in Scotland, scene of the 1314 battle when Robert the Bruce routed the English, Stirling.
Ben Lawers, Perthshire mountain reserve with views to North Sea.
Ben Lomond, rising to 3,200ft from east shore of Loch Lomond.
Blackhill, Iron Age hill fort, near Lanark.
Boath Dovecot, site of ancient motte, Nairn.
Brodick Castle, 13th century castle on ancient Viking fortress isle, Isle of Arran.
Goatfell, highest peak on Arran.
Brodie Castle, family home since 1160, Forres, near Inverness.
Bruce's Stone, granite boulder marks where Bruce defeated English in 1307, near New Galloway.
Bucinch and Ceardach, uninhabited islands in Loch Lomond.
Burg, cliffs known as 'The Wilderness', Isle of Mull.
Caiy Stone, site of battle between Picts and Romans, Edinburgh.
Canna, most westerly of the so-called Small isles, Hebrides.
Castle Campbell, imposing 15th century chief's home, in Dollar **Glen**, Clackmannanshire (under guardianship of Historic Scotland).
Clava Cairns, 2000 BC, near Inverness (under guardianship of Historic Scotland).
Castle Fraser, magnificent 16th century turrets, Inverurie, near Aberdeen.
Corrieshalloch Gorge, box canyon near Ullapool.
Craigievar Castle, 17th century 'fairytale' castle, Alford, near Aberdeen.
Craigower, beacon hill near Pitlochry.
Crathes Castle, lands granted by the Bruce surround 16th century castle, Banchory, near Aberdeen.
Crookston Castle, 15th century, Glasgow (under guardianship of Historic Scotland).
Culloden, site of last battle on British soil, Jacobite Rebellion ended here 1746, east of Inverness.
Culross Palace, 16th century, Fife.
Direlton Castle, beautiful ruins dating from 1225, near North Berwick, Lothian (under guardianship of Historic Scotland).
Drum Castle, one of three oldest tower houses in Scotland, begun 13th century, near Aberdeen.
Dunkeld, large areas of old village, Perth & Kinross.
Fair Isle, isolated inhabited island, Shetland.
Falkland Palace, country residence of Stewart Kings, Fife.
Falls of Glomach, Kyle of Lochalsh.
Finavon Dovecot, largest dovecot in Scotland, 2,400 nesting boxes, 16th century, Forfar.
Fyvie Castle, grandest example of Scottish baronial architecture, 13th century, Aberdeenshire.
Gladstone's Land, 17th century tenement, Edinburgh.
Glencoe and Dalness, historic glen and scene of 1692 massacre, Highlands.
Glenfinnan Monument, Loch Shiel, near Fort William.
Glenluce Abbey, 12th century Cistercian, Dumfries & Galloway (under guardianship of Historic Scotland).
Grey Mare's Tail, spectacular waterfall near Moffat, Dumfries & Galloway.
Hamilton House, 17th century home of prosperous Edinburgh merchant, and adjacent 15th century Preston Tower, Prestonpans, Lothian.
House of the Binns, 17th century mansion, Linlithgow, Lothian.
Hugh Miller's Cottage, 17th century, Cromarty.
Iona, 1,800 acres of the island where St Columba arrived in 563 AD.
Kellie Castle, 14th and 16th century, Pittenweem, Fife.
Killiecrankie, pastoral reserve close to 1689 battle site, Pitlochry.
Kintail and Morvich, magnificent stretch of West Highland scenery, near Kyle of Lochalsh.
Lamb's House, 16th century home of prosperous Edinburgh merchant, Leith.
Leith Hall, family estate since 1650, Huntly, north of Aberdeen.
Linn of Tummel, characteristic beauty of Perthshire Highlands, near Pitlochry.
Mar Lodge Estate, 77,500 acres containing four of the ten highest mountains in the British Isles, Ballater, Aberdeenshire.
Pitmedden Garden, laid out in 1675, Ellon, Aberdeenshire.
Provan Hall, 15th century, the most perfect pre-Reformation mansion house in Scotland, Glasgow.
Provost Ross's House, 16th century, overlooking harbour, is one of oldest houses in Aberdeen.
St Abb's Head, spectacular headland, Borders.
St Kilda, remote, dramatic and now uninhabited archipelago 110 miles out into Atlantic.
Scotstarvit Tower, fine 16th century tower house, Cupar, Fife (under guardianship of Historic Scotland).
Staffa, island of Fingal's Cave, immortalised by Mendelssohn, west of Mull.
Strome Castle, 15th century stronghold of the Lords of the Isles, Loch Carron, Highlands.
Threave Castle, 14th century stronghold in island in River Dee, Dumfries & Galloway (under guardianship of Historic Scotland).
Torridon, 16,100 acres of Scotland's finest mountain scenery (including Shieldaig Island, in Loch Torridon), Highlands.
Turret House, opposite Kelso Abbey, Borders.
West Affric, 9,000 acres of wild landscapes, near Cannich, Highlands.

By joining the National Trust For Scotland, you will help preserve the fine examples of Scotland's rich, architectural, scenic and historic heritage which are in its care. You can join Scotland's leading conservation organisation at its headquarters at 5 Charlotte Square, Edinburgh EH2 4DU or at any of its properties. Ordinary membership is £25, family membership is £42.

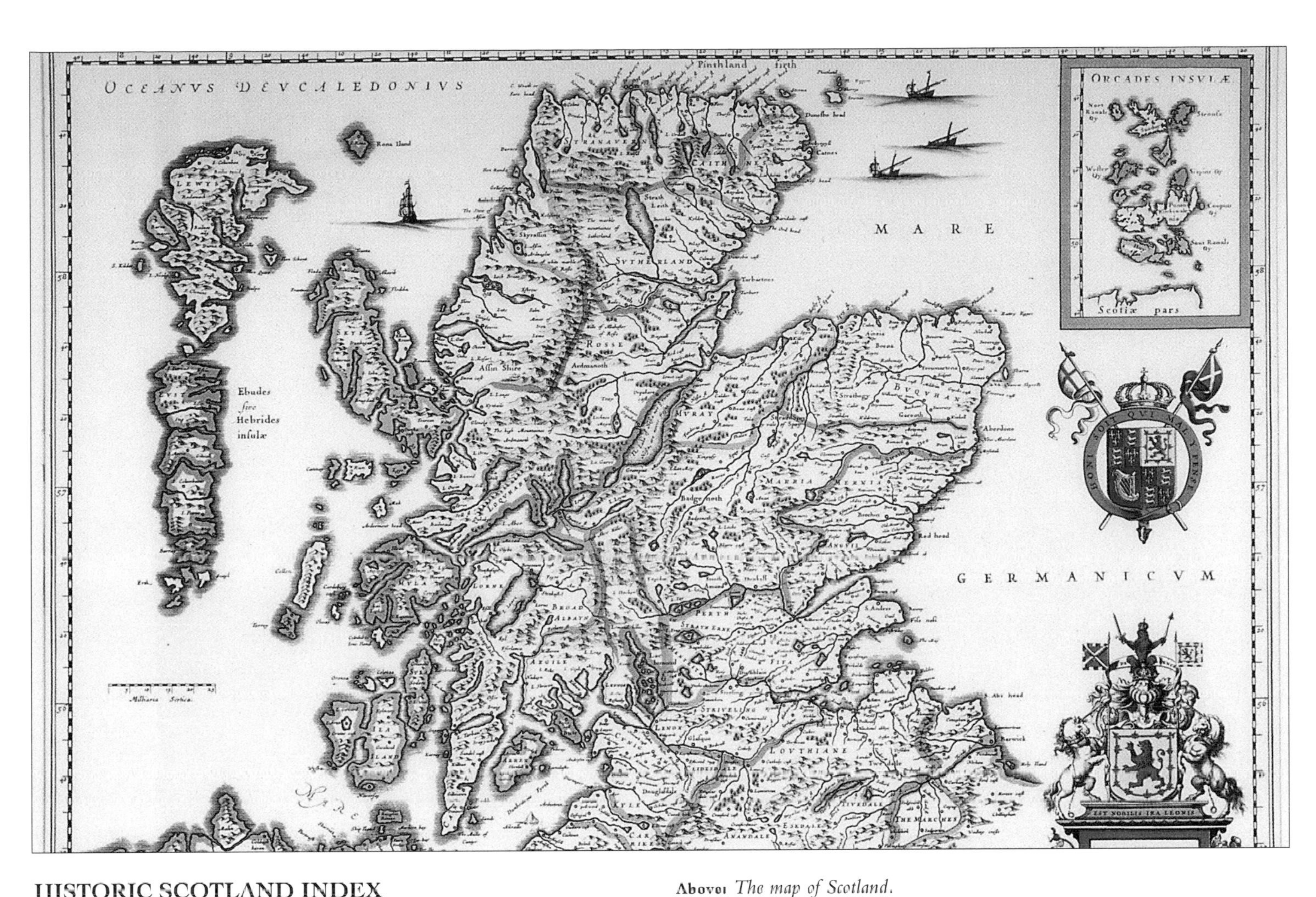

Above: *The map of Scotland.*

HISTORIC SCOTLAND INDEX

Scenes and sites of Ancient Scotland
cared for by Historic Scotland
(Longmore House, Salisbury Place, Edinburgh EH9 1SH)

Aberdour Castle, 14th century fortified residence, Fife & Central.
Aberlemno Sculptured Stones, in churchyard near near Forfar, Tayside.
Abernethy Round Tower, 11th century, Tayside.
Achnabreck Cup and Ring Marks, Bronze Age, at Poltalloch, near Lochgilphead, Argyll & Bute.
Arbroath Abbey, 12th century ruins, Tayside.
Ardchattan Priory, 13th century, near Oban.
Ardclach Bell Tower, 17th century, near Nairn, Inverness.
Ardestie Earth-house, Iron Age, near Arbroath.
Ardunie Roman Signal Station, near Auchterarder.
Argyll Lodging, 17th century, Stirling.
Auchagallon Stone Circle, Bronze Age burial cairn, Isle of Arran.
Ballygowan Cup and Ring Marks and Balluachraig Cup & Ring Marks, Bronze Age, near Poltalloch, Highlands.
Balvaird Castle, 15th century, Bridge of Earn.
Balvenie Castle, 13th century, Dufftown.
Bar Hill Fort, on the Antonine Wall.
Barochan Cross, Celtic cross in Paisley Abbey.
Barsalloch Fort, Iron Age hill fort, Dumfries and Galloway.
Bearsden Roman Bathhouse, 2nd century AD.
Beauly Priory, 13th century.
Bishop's and Earl's Palaces, 13th century-plus, Kirkwall, Orkney.
Blackfriars Chapel, Dominican friars' church, St Andrews.
Blackhall Roman Camps, Tayside.
Blackhammer Chambered Cairn, Neolithic, Orkney.
Blackhouse, thatched house, Arnol, Isle of Lewis.
Blackness Castle, 15th century, Linlithgow.
Bothwell Castle, largest 13th century stone castle in Scotland, overlooking the Clyde.
Brandsbutt Symbol Stone, Pictish stone, near Inverurie.
Brechin Cathedral Round Tower, 11th century, Tayside.
Brough of Birsay, Norse church and village ruins, Orkney.
Broch of Gurness, Orkney.
Broughty Castle, 16th century tower, Dundee.
Burghead Well, early Christian baptistry, Grampian.
Burleigh Castle, roofless ruin c1500, Tayside.
Caerlaverock Castle, splendid Renaissance castle, near Dumfries.
Cairnbaan Cup and Ring Marks, near Lochgilphead.
Cairn Holy Chambered Cairns, Neolithic burial chambers, Dumfries and Galloway.
Cairn o'Get, burial chamber, Lybster.

Cairnpapple Hill, burial site from 3000 to 1400 BC, Lothian.
Callanish Standing Stones, near Stornoway, Lewis.
Cambuskenneth Abbey, in 1326 Robert Bruce's parliament, Stirling.
Cardoness Castle, 15th century, Gatehouse-of-Fleet.
Carlungie Earth-house, Iron Age, Tayside.
Carnasserie Castle, 16th century, Argyll & Bute.
Carn Ban, Neolithic cairn, Arran.
Carn Liath, broch near Golspie, Sutherland.
Carsluith Castle, 16th century, Dumfries & Galloway.
Castle Campbell, 15th century, near Dollar, Tayside (National Trust for Scotland property under the guardianship of Historic Scotland).
Castlecary, earthworks, Fife & Central.
Castlelaw Hill Fort, Iron Age, Lothian.
Castle of Old Wick, Norse Tower House, Caithness.
Castle Sween, 12th century, Argyll & Bute.
Caterthuns, hill forts near Brechin, Tayside.
Chapel Finian, c1000 AD, Dumfries & Galloway.
Chesters Hill Fort, Iron Age fort and ramparts, Lothian.
Church of St Magnus, 12th century, Orkney.
Clackmannan Tower, 14th century tower house overlooking Forth.
Clava Cairns, Stone Age-Bronze Age stone circles, Inverness (National Trust for Scotland property under the guardianship of Historic Scotland).
Claypotts Castle, 16th century, Tayside.
Clickhimin Broch, Iron Age tower, Lerwick.
Cnoc Freiceadain Long Cairns, Neolithic, Thurso.
Corgarff Castle, 16th century tower house, Grampian.
Corrimony Chambered Cairn, Glen Urquhart, near Drumnadrochit.
Coulter Motte, Norman castle mound, South Strathclyde.
Craigmillar Castle, 15th century, Edinburgh.
Craignethan Castle, 16th century, near Lanark.
Crichton Castle, built by the Earl of Bothwell, 16th century, Lothian.
Crookston Castle, 15th century, Glasgow (National Trust for Scotland property under the guardianship of Historic Scotland).
Cross Kirk, Peebles, 13th century.
Crossraguel Abbey, 13th century, South Strathclyde.
Cubbie Row's Castle, built by Norsemen around 1145, Wyre, Orkney.
Cullerlie Stone Circle, 2000 BC, Aberdeen.
Culross Abbey, 13th century, Firth of Forth.
Culsh Earth-house, 2,000 years old, Grampian.
Cuween Hill Chambered Cairn, Neolithic, near Kirkwall.
Deer Abbey, Cistercian ruins, near Peterhead.
Deskford Church, late-medieval, near Cullen, Grampian.
Dirleton Castle, beautiful 13th century ruins, Lothian (National Trust for Scotland property under the guardianship of Historic Scotland).
Doonhill Homestead, site of hall of a 6th century chief, near Dunbar.

Right: *St Clement's church, Rodel, Isle of Harris.*

Doune Castle, 14th century.
Druchtag Motte, 12th century castle, Dumfries & Galloway.
Drumcoltran Tower, 16th century, Dumfries & Galloway.
Drumtroddan Cup and Ring Marks and Standing Stones, Bronze Age carvings and stones, Dumfries & Galloway.
Dryburgh Abbey, magnificent 12th century, Borders.
Duffus Castle, fine motte castle, near Elgin.
Dumbarton Castle, ancient capital of Strathclyde.
Dunadd Fort, spectacular stronghold of Scots kingdom of **Dalriada**, Argyll & Bute.
Dun Beag Broch, occupied until 18th century, Skye.
Dunblane Cathedral, noble medieval church.
Dun Carloway Broch, beautifully preserved, Lewis.
Dunchraigaig Cairn, Bronze Age, Argyll & Bute.
Dundonald Castle, large structure on site of prehistoric hill fort, South Strathclyde.
Dun Dornaigil Broch, Sutherland.
Dundrennan Abbey, Cistercian founded 12th century, near Kirkcudbright.
Dunfermline Abbey and Palace, 11th century Benedictine abbey and palace birthplace of Charles I.
Dunfallandy Stone, Pictish sculpture, Pitlochry.
Dunglass Collegiate Church, 15th century, Lothian.
Dunkeld Cathedral, 15th century, on banks of Tay.
Dunstaffnage Castle and Chapel, 13th century, Oban.
Dwarfie Stane, Neolithic burial chamber, Orkney.
Dyce Symbol Stones, Pictish carvings in ruined parish church of Dyce, Grampian.
Earl's Palace, Birsay, 16th century palace of Earl of Orkney.
Eassie Sculptured Stone, in Eassie church, near Glamis, Tayside.
Easter Aquhorthies Stone Circle, 2000 AD, near Inverurie, Grampian.
Eileach an Naoimh, island associated with St Columba, north of Jura.
Eilean Mor, island with 12th century chapel, in Sound of Jura.
Edinburgh Castle, the most famous in Scotland.
Edin's Hall Broch, Iron Age, near Granthouse, Borders.
Edrom Church, Norman doorway, near Duns.
Edzell Castle, 16th century, near Brechin,Tayside.
Elcho Castle, complete 16th century mansion, on Tay.
Elgin Cathedral, 13th century superb ruin.
Eynhallow Church, 12th century, Orkney.
Fort Charlotte, 1665 artillery fort, Lerwick, Shetland.
Fortrose Cathedral, 13th century, near Inverness.
Glasgow Cathedral, only medieval mainland cathedral to have survived Reformation complete.
Glebe Cairn, Bronze Age burial chambers, Argyll & Bute.
Glenbuchat Castle, 16th century, Grampian.
Glenelg Brochs, two towers in beautiful setting, Kyle of Lochalsh.
Glenluce Abbey, 1192, Cistercian, Dumfries & Galloway (National Trust for Scotland property under the guardianship of Historic Scotland).
Grain Earth-house, near Kirkwall, Orkney.
Greenknowe Tower, 16th century, near Gordon, Borders.
Greay Cairns of Camster, Neolithic burial chambers, Lybster, Caithness.

Hailes Castle, 13th century, Lothian.
Hermitage Castle, 14th century ruin, near Hawick, Borders.
Holm of Papa Westray Chambered Cairn, massive tomb, Orkney.
Holyrood Abbey and Park, 12th century, of Augustinian order, adjacent to Palace of Holyrood.
Huntingtower Castle, 15th century, Perth.
Huntly Castle, 12th century motte, beautiful setting, Grampian.
Inchcolm Abbey, 1123, best preserved monastic buildings in Scotland, on isle in Firth of Firth.
Inchkenneth Chapel, medieval, off Mull.
Inchmahome Priory, 13th century Augustinian, in Lake Menteith, Fife & Central.
Innerpeffray Chapel, 16th century, near Crieff, Tayside.
Inverlochy Castle, finely preserved 13th century, near Fort William.
Jarlshof, amazing prehistoric and Norse settlement, Shetland.
Jedburgh Abbey, magnificent ruins from 1138, Borders.
Kelso Abbey, 1128, beautiful but less well preserved, Borders.
Kilchurn Castle, 16th century with spectacular views of Loch Awe.
Kildalton Cross, 9th century finest high cross in Scotland, Isle of Islay.
Kildrummy Castle, 13th century, Grampian.
Kilmartin Sculptured Stones, grave slabs in parish church, Argyll & Bute.
Kilmory Knap Chapel, medieval church with grave slabs, Loch Sween, Argyll & Bute.
Kilwinning Abbey, 13th century ruins, South Strathclyde.
King's Knot, formal 17th century gardens, beneath Stirling
Kinkell Church, 16th century ruins, Inverurie, Grampian.
Kinneil House, 15th century tower, Bo'ness, Fife & Central.
Kirkmadrine Early Christian Stones, 5th century, earliest Christian memorial stones, Sandhead, Dumfries & Galloway.
Knap of Howar, Neolithic, oldest standing stone houses in north-west Europe, Orkney.
Knowe of Yarso Chambered Cairn, Neolithic, Rousay, Orkney.
Largs Old Kirk, elaborate 17th century monument.
Lauderdale Aisle, St Mary's, remains of great 15th century church, Haddington, Lothian.
Lincluden Collegiate Church, 14th century, Dumfries.
Linlithgow Palace, magnificent ruin, birthplace of Mary Queen of Scots and James V, Lothian.
Loanhead Stone Circle, 2000 BC-plus, Grampian.
Loch Doon Castle, 700-year-old masonry amazingly transplanted from original island site in the 1930s, South Strathclyde
Lochleven Castle, 14th century jail of Mary Queen of Scots on island in Loch Leven, Tayside.
Lochmaben Castle, 14th century, Dumfries & Galloway.
Lochranza Castle, 16th century, Isle of Arran.
Machrie Moor Stone Circles, Bronze Age, Isle of Arran.
MacLean's Cross, 15th century standing stone, island of Iona.
MacLellan's Castle, 16th century, Kirkcudbright.
Maes Howe Chambered Cairn, finest Megalithic tomb in the British Isles, near Kirkwall, Orkney.
Maiden Stone, 9th century Pictish carved slab, Garioch, Grampian.
Maison Dieu Chapel, medieval hospital, Brechin, Tayside.
Mar's Wark, 1570 Renaissance mansion, Stirling.
Meigle Sculptured Stone Museum, 25 monuments, Tayside.
Melrose Abbey, 1136 Cistercian abbey, most famed ruin in Scotland, Borders.
Memsie Cairn, Bronze Age, near Rathen, Grampian.
Midhowe Broch and Chambered Cairn, huge and impressive
Megalithic monument, on Rousay island, Orkney.
Morton Castle, 13th century hall house, Dumfries & Galloway.
Mousa Broch, superb surviving Iron Age broch tower, Shetland.
Muir o'Fauld Roman Signal Station, watch tower site, Ardunie, Tayside.
Muness Castle, 16th century tower house, Unst, Shetland.
Muthill Old Church and Tower, 15th century, Crieff, Tayside.
Ness of Burgi, Iron Age block house, Scatness, Shetland.
Nether Largie Cairns, Neolithic and Bronze Age, Argyll & Bute.
Newark Castle, 15th century, Port Glasgow.
Noltland Castle, 16th century unfinished, Westray, Orkney.
Orchardton Tower, unique circular 15th century tower, Dumfries & Galloway.
Ormiston Market Cross, 15th century, Lothian.
Orphir-Earl's Bu and Church, 12th century and earlier Viking ruins, near Kirkwall, Orkney.
Peel Ring of Lumphanan, 13th century defensive earthwork, Grampian.
Picardy Symbol Stone, one of oldest Pictish stones, perhaps 7th century, near Mireton, Grampian.
Pierowall Church, medieval, Westray, Orkney.
Preston Market Cross, elaborate 17th century monument, Lothian.
Quoyness Chambered Cairn, Megalithic and Neolithic, Sanday, Orkney.
Ravenscraig Castle, royal artillery fort, Kirkcaldy, Fife.
Rennibister Earth-house, near Kirkwall, Orkney.
Restenneth Priory, Augustinian, near Forfar, Tayside.
Ring of Brogar Stone Circle and Henge, magnificent circle of standing stones with ditches, Stromness, Orkney.
Rothesay Castle, 13th century residence of Stewart kings, Isle of Bute.
Rough Castle, best preserved ramparts of Antonine Wall, near Bonnybridge, Fife & Central (this and two other sections of the Antonine Wall are National Trust for Scotland properties under the guardianship of Historic Scotland).
Ruthven Barracks, burned by Jacobites in 1746, near Kingussie.
Ruthwell Cross, 7th century Anglican cross, one of major Dark Age monuments in Europe, near Dumfries.
St Andrews Castle, ruins from 13th century, Fife & Central.
St Andrews Cathedral and St Rule's Tower, remains of largest cathedral in Scotland, early 12th century.
St Blane's Church, Kingart, site of Celtic monastery, Isle of Bute.
St Bride's Church, Douglas, 14th century, South Strathclyde.
St Bridget's Church, Dalgety, medieval church on banks of Forth.

Right: *Edinburgh Castle.*

St Clement's Church, Rodel, 16th century, Isle of Harris.
St Machar's Cathedral Transepts, 16th century ruins, Aberdeen.
St Martin's Church, Haddington, 13th century ruins, Lothian.
St Mary's Chapel, Crosskirk, simple, 12th century chapel, near Thurso, Caithness.
St Mary's Chapel, Rothesay, late-medieval remains, Argyll & Bute.
St Mary's Church, Grandtully, 16th century, near Aberfeldy, Tayside.
St Mary's Kirk, Auchindoir, one of finest medieval parish churches in Scotland, near Lumsden, Grampian.
St Ninian's Cave, early crosses found here, near Whithorn, Dumfries & Galloway.
St Ninian's Chapel, 13th century pilgrims' chapel, Isle of Whithorn, Dumfries & Galloway.
St Peter's Kirk and Parish Cross, Duffus, 14th century, Grampian.
St Tridiuana's Chapel, James III's unique shrine to Pictish saint, in Restalrig Collegiate Church, Edinburgh.
St Vigean's Sculptured Stones, 32 early Pictish and Christian stones, Arbroath, Tayside.
Scalloway Castle, built 1600, Shetland.
Scotstarvit Tower, 16th century, Cupar, Fife (National Trust for Scotland property under the guardianship of Historic Scotland).
Seton Collegiate Church, 15th century, Lothian.
Skara Brae Prehistoric Village, best preserved Stone Age houses in Western Europe, Shetland.
Skipness Castle and Chapel, 13th century, Kintyre.
Smailholm Tower, impressive rectangular tower near Kelso, Borders.
Spynie Palace, 14th century, Elgin, Grampian.
Staneydale 'Temple', Neolithic hall, near Walls, Shetland.
Steinacleit Cairn and Stone Circle, enigmatic prehistoric ruins, near Stornaway, isle of Lewis.
Stirling Castle, second most famous castle in Scotland and arguably the grandest.
Stirling Old Bridge, dating from 15th century, with Jacobite connections.
Stones of Stenness Circle and Henge, Stromness, Orkney.
Sueno's Stone, 20ft high, claimed to be one of the most remarkable sculptured monuments in Britain, Forres, Grampian.
Sweetheart Abbey, ruin in 30 acres, 13th century monument by Lady of Galloway in memory of her husband, near Dumfries.
Tantallon Castle, remarkable 14th century fortification dramatically situated on promontory near North Berwichk.
Tarves Medieval Tomb, near Aberdeen.
Taversöe Tuick Chambered Cairn, Megalithic and Neolithic, Stromness, Orkney.
Tealing Dovecot and Earth-house, Iron Age earth-house and elegant 16th century dovecot, near Dundee.
Threave Castle, 14th century tower on island, near Castle Douglas, Dumfries & Galloway (National Trust for Scotland property under the guardianship of Historic Scotland).
Tolquhon Castle, 15th century, near Aberdeen.
Tomnaverie Stone Circle, 2000 BC, Aboyne, Grampian.
Torhouse Stone Circle, Bronze Age, Wigtown, Dumfries & Galloway.
Torr a'Chaisteal Fort, Iron Age fort, near Blackwaterfoot, Arran.
Torrylin Cairn, Neolithic, near Lagg, Arran.
Tullibardine Chapel, complete and unaltered medieval church, near Crieff, Tayside.
Unstan Chambered Cairn, Neolithic, Stromness, Orkney.
Urquhart Castle, beautiful ruins from several ages, dramatically sited on a promontory overlooking Loch Ness.
Watling Lodge, best section of ditch of Antonine Wall, Falkirk.
West Port, 16th century city gate of St Andrews.
Westquarter Dovecot, 17th century, near Lauriston, Fife & Central.
Westside Church, Tuquoy, 12th century, Westray, Orkney.
Whithorn Priory and Museum, cradle of Christianity in Scotland, founded in the 5th century as St Ninian's 'Shining Light'.
Wideford Hill Chambered Cairn, Neolithic, near Kirkwall, Orkney.

By becoming a 'Friend Of Historic Scotland', you will be preserving the nation's heritage and helping to protect more than 300 buildings, monuments and other priceless properties. Membership means free admission to them all — and the knowledge that you are supporting a team of archaeologists, historians, architects and conservators in preserving these historical gems for future generations. For membership details, write to Historic Scotland at: Longmore House, Salisbury Place, Edinburgh EH9 1SH.